Pierre Poivre

The Travels of a Philosopher

Being observations on the customs, manners, arts, of several nations in Asia and Africa

Pierre Poivre

The Travels of a Philosopher
Being observations on the customs, manners, arts, of several nations in Asia and Africa

ISBN/EAN: 9783337315245

Printed in Europe, USA, Canada, Australia, Japan

Cover: Foto ©Andreas Hilbeck / pixelio.de

More available books at www.hansebooks.com

TRAVELS
OF A
PHILOSOPHER:
OR,
OBSERVATIONS
ON THE
MANNERS AND ARTS
OF
VARIOUS NATIONS
IN
AFRICA AND ASIA.

TRANSLATED
FROM THE FRENCH OF M. LE POIVRE,
LATE ENVOY TO THE KING OF COCHIN-
CHINA, AND NOW INTENDANT OF THE
ISLES OF BOURBON AND MAURITIUS.

DUBLIN:
Printed for P. and W. WILSON, J. EXSHAW, H. SAUNDERS, W. SLEATER, B. GRIERSON, D. CHAMBERLAINE, J. HOEY, jun. and J. WILLIAMS, M DCC LXX.

ADVERTISEMENT.

LES VOYAGES D'UN PHILOSOPHE of M. le Poivre have been much admired in France. They were originally read in 1764 and 1765, before the Royal Society of Agriculture at Lyons, of which he was then prefident, and afterwards before the Royal Society of Paris in 1766. For fome time they were handed about in manufcript, and at length, in 1768, found their way to the prefs.

M. le Poivre's manner is easy and elegant; his observations striking and judicious; his sentiments philanthropical and benevolent.—The genuine happiness of every nation must depend on agriculture, and agriculture must ever be influenced by established laws and modes of government: nature indulgently smiles on the labour of a free-born people, but shrinks with horror from the tyrant and the slave. This is his system, and it is the system of truth founded on experience, and supported not only by by comparing cotemporary nations, but by contrasting nations with themselves at different periods.

It is neceſſary the reader ſhould keep in view the country of the author, as many of his ſtrictures on European agriculture, though unapplicable perhaps to Britain, convey a deſcriptive Picture of the ſtate of cultivation in France.

Originals generally ſuffer by tranſlation : this obſervation perhaps, with too great juſtice, may

may be applied to the prefent attempt. As a gentleman, however, will be diftinguifhed in any garb, it is hoped M. le Poivre's intrinfic merit will procure him a polite reception, whatever impropriety or inelegance may be found in his prefent drefs.

CONTENTS.

Introduction	Page 1
The western Coast of Africa	6
The Cape of Good Hope	9
Madagascar	20
Isle of Bourbon	27
Isle of France	30
Coast of Coromandel	36
Machine for watering rice grounds	40
Mode of labour	42
Flocks of sheep, &c.	43
Gardens	45
The Cocoa-tree	46
The kingdom of Siam	51
The Malais	64
Sagou	74

PART SECOND.

Power of agriculture — Origin of the kingdom of Ponthiamas — 90

Camboya

CONTENTS.

Camboya and Tsiampa — 98
Cochin-china — — 100
   Culture of different kinds of rice in Cochin-china — 103
   Sugar-canes — — 110
China — — — 137
   Ceremony of opening the grounds 162
   Encouragements of agriculture 166
   Attention of the Chinese government — — 168
   The imposts established in China invariable — — 170
   The impost called the tenth 171
   Comparison of the agriculture of Africa and Asia with that of China — — 174
The state of agriculture in Europe 176
                 in Africa 177
                 in America 178
                 in Asia 179

TRAVELS

OF A

PHILOSOPHER.

EVERY people, however barbarous, have arts peculiar to themſelves. The diverſity of climates, whilſt it varies the wants of mankind, offers to their induſtry different productions on which to exercife it. Every country, at a certain degree of diſtance, has fabrics ſo ſingularly peculiar to itſelf, that they could not have been the fabrics of other regions : but agriculture, in every climate, is the univerſal art of mankind : from one extreme of the globe to the other, nations ſtill barbarous, as well as thoſe whoſe ideas are civilized, procure to them-
A ſelves

felves, at leaſt, a part of their ſubſiſtence by the culture of their fields; yet this art, however univerſal, is not every where equally flouriſhing.

It never fails to proſper among wiſe nations, who know how to honour and encourage it;—it ſupports itſelf but feebly amongſt a people half poliſhed, who either prefer to it frivolous arts, or who, being ſufficiently enlightened perhaps to perceive its utility, are ſtill too much ſlaves to the prejudices of their ancient barbarity, to affranchize and confer honours on thoſe who exerciſe it;—it languiſhes, and its influence is ſcarcely to be obſerved amongſt barbarians, who deſpiſe it.

The ſtate of agriculture has ever been the principal object of my re-
ſearches

searches among the various people I have seen in the course of my voyages. It is almost impossible for a traveller, who perhaps only passes through a country, to make such remarks as are necessary to convey a just idea of the government, police, and manners of the inhabitants. In such a case, the criterion which best marks the internal state of a nation, is to observe the public markets, and the face of the country. If the markets abound in provisions, if the fields are well cultivated, and covered with rich crops, then in general you may conclude that the country is well peopled, that the inhabitants are civilized and happy, that their manners are polished, and their government agreeable to the principles of reason.—You may then say to yourself, I am amongst *Men*.

When, on the contrary, I have arrived amongſt a people, whom it was neceſſary to ſearch for amidſt foreſts, whoſe neglected lands were overgrown with brambles; when I have traverſed large tracts of uncultivated deſarts, and then at laſt ſtumbled on a grubb'd-up wretchedly cultivated field; when arrived at length at ſome canton, I have obſerved nothing in the public market but a few ſorry roots; I no longer heſitated to determine the inhabitants to be wretched ſavages, or groaning under the moſt oppreſſive ſlavery.

I never remember a ſingle inſtance of being obliged to retract this firſt idea, conceived ſimply by inſpecting the ſtate of agriculture amongſt the various nations I have ſeen: the knowledge

ledge of various particulars, which a long refidence amongft many of them has enabled me to acquire, has ever confirmed me in opinion, that a country poorly cultivated is always inhabited by men barbarous or opprefled, and that population there can never be confiderable.

You will obferve by the detail I now offer you of my enquiries, that in every country agriculture depends abfolutely on the laws, the manners and even on the eftablifhed prejudices of the refpective inhabitants. I fhall begin with obfervations on fome parts of Africa.

THE WESTERN COASTS OF AFRICA.

The iflands and weftern diftricts of this part of the world which I have feen, are for the greater part uncultivated lands, inhabited by unhappy negroes. Thefe wretched men, who have fo poor an eftimation of themfelves as to fell one another, never employ a thought on the cultivation of their lands. Satisfied to exift from day to day, under a climate where their wants are few, they cultivate juft as much as prevents their dying of hunger; they carelefsly fow every year fome maize, a very little rice, and plant in fmall quantities, different kinds of potatoes, not of the nature of ours, though the culture is much the fame; we know them

them by the name of *yams*. In general their harvests are so poor, that the Europeans, who resort to them for the purchase of slaves, are obliged to bring from Europe or America the provisions necessary for the maintenance of those unfortunate creatures doomed to compose their cargoes.

The negroes who inhabit the environs of the European colonies, give somewhat more attention to agriculture than the others. — They rear flocks; they cultivate rice in greater quantities; and in their gardens are found pulse, of which the seed has been brought from Europe; yet all they know of agriculture, they have learnt from the Europeans settled amongst them; their own experience is extremely bounded; and I have never been able to discover in their induſtry any proceſs which could in the leaſt improve our own.

From the river of Angola to Cape Negroe, and from thence till you approach the Cape of Good Hope, nothing is to be ſeen but ſterile uncultivated lands; the coaſts are naked, and covered with barren ſands; and you are under the neceſſity of travelling many leagues before you can diſcover a palm-tree, or the ſlighteſt verdure. The country and its few inhabitants ſeem to be ſtruck with one common curſe. From the informations I have received touching theſe countries from the Italian miſſionaries, who with an admirable zeal have penetrated into the heart of theſe accurſed regions, I learn likewiſe that agriculture is juſt as languid in the interior parts as upon the

the coafts, although, in many places, the foil appeared much more fruitful from its natural productions.

THE CAPE OF GOOD HOPE.

The countries around the Cape were condemned to the fame fterility before the Dutch took poffeffion of them; but fince their eftablifhment on this point of Africa, the lands produce in abundance wheat and grain of every kind, wines of different qualities, and a confiderable quantity of excellent fruits, collected from every quarter of the world. There you fee extenfive paftures covered with horfes, black cattle, and fheep—thefe herds and flocks thrive exceedingly well. The abundance which this colony enjoys, compared to the barrennefs of the furrounding countries, evidently

dently demonſtrates that the earth denies her favours only to the tyrant and the ſlave; but becomes prodigal of her treaſures, beyond the moſt ſanguine hope ſo ſoon as ſhe is free, and cultivated by men of diſcernment, whom wiſe and invariable laws protect.

A number of Frenchmen, forced from their country by the revocation of the edict of Nantz, have on this coaſt found a new eſtabliſhment, and with it, ſecurity, property, and liberty, the only true encouragers of agriculture, the only principles of abundance. They have enriched this adopted mother by their induſtry; they have there founded conſiderable colonies, ſome of which bear the name of that unhappy country which denied them the uſe of water and of fire,

fire, the remembrance of which however they ſtill fondly cheriſh.

The colony of Little Rochelle ſurpaſſes all the reſt, by the induſtry of the coloniſts, and the fertility of the lands which belong to it. The paſtures are there compoſed of a variety of graſſes, natives of the country, together with ſeveral different ſpecies of herbage, which compoſe our artificial meadows in Europe, ſuch as trefoil, lucerne, and faintfoin. The exotic plants, the ſeeds of which have been imported by the Dutch, flouriſh there as the natural productions of the country. Thoſe ſeeds are ſown by an operation of the plough; they cut the graſs only the firſt year; the ſecond they open the meadows to cattle, which live there at diſcretion, without any other attention than that of collecting

lecting them together every evening into a park inclofed with ftrong and high pallifadoes, to fecure them againft the lions and tigers, with which this country abounds.

Some of thefe enclofures are watered only by the rains, although they generally endeavour to choofe them in the neighbourhood of fome brook, where they dig commodious watering places. In all thefe pafturages, they have an eye to groves of trees, where the herds and flocks may find fhelter againft the intenfe heat of the fun; particularly in January, February, and March, which in this part of the world are the moft fultry months in the year.

The arable land is here laboured as in Europe, fometimes by horfes,
but

but oftener by oxen : the Dutch of this colony have by their induſtry corrected the natural ſluggiſhneſs of theſe latter animals, by exerciſing them while young in a briſk pace; in conſequence of which I have ſeen, at the Cape, carriages, drawn by teams of ten or a dozen yoke of oxen, go as expeditiouſly as if drawn by horſes.

The grains commonly ſown at the Cape, are wheat, turkey corn, and rice; theſe generally produce an increaſe of fifty-fold. They cultivate a variety of different kinds of pulſe, ſuch as peaſe, common beans, and French beans. This pulſe makes a refreſhing proviſion to the ſhips touching at the Cape going or returning to India.

A particular ſpecies of this pulſe is much in requeſt in India, to which they

they export a confiderable quantity: it is there known by the name of *Cape Peafe:* it is a kind of French bean which requires no prop; its grain is of the form of that bean, but larger and flatter; it taftes like our green peafe, and preferves its frefhnefs for a long time. I have this year attempted the culture of this plant, which promifes fuccefs. The climate at the Cape feems to demand from the cultivator an attention which appears not fo neceffary in this country, and which would even perhaps be prejudicial to the productions of our lands.

The Cape however is expofed the greateft part of the year to violent hurricanes, which blow generally from the north-eaft. Thefe winds are fo impetuous that they would

beat

beat down the fruits from the trees, and fweep to deftruction the labours of the farmer, had they not provided a barrier for the fecurity of the harveft. The Dutch colonifts have divided their lands into fmall fields, which they have furrounded with high pallifades of oaks and other trees, planted very clofe to one another, fomewhat refembling a charmille, defigned for the ornament of a garden. Thefe pallifades they cut every year, as they grow; their heighth being commonly from twenty-five to thirty feet; every feparate field, in confequence, is enclofed like a chamber.

It is by this induftry alone that the Dutch have rendered this colony not only the granary of all their fettlements in the Eaft-Indies, but the

moft

moſt commodious place for veſſels to touch at for refreſhments and proviſions of all kinds.

When the dutch began to form their vineyards, they endeavoured to procure plants from thoſe cantons which enjoyed the greateſt reputation for their vines; but after many fruitleſs attempts to produce, at the extremity of Africa, the wines of Burgundy and Champagne, they applied to rearing the plants tranſported from Spain, the Canaries, and the Levant, where the climate is more analagous to the Cape. At preſent the plants which are cultivated moſt ſuccefsfully, are thoſe of the Muſcadel kind: the red Muſcadel particularly, which they rear in a ſmall diſtrict called Conſtance, produces moſt delicious wine; the Dutch Eaſt-India Company

Company always secure this vintage, which they send in presents to the sovereigns of Europe.

The wines at the Cape are cultivated without vine-props; the method of labour is much the same with that in France. The vineyards are surrounded by a number of trees, upon which they entwine the slips of the great Spanish Muscadine, in form of espaliers, very high, by which the vines are sheltered from the violence of the winds.

The same attention, at the Cape, is paid to gardening, as to the other branches of agriculture. You there find all the variety of European pulse, greens, herbs, and roots, with the best of those peculiar to other parts of the world. Independent of the

gardens

gardens of the colonifts, which are kept in as fine order as any in Europe, the India Company have caufed to be laid out two or three gardens, extenfive and magnificent, which they fupport with an expence worthy of a fovereign company.

Fifteen or twenty European gardeners, whofe abilities are approved before they are embarked, are employed in the cultivation of each of thofe vaft gardens, under the direction of a principal gardener, whofe place is lucrative and honourable. It is in thofe gardens, at the expence of the company, that all the experiments are made in every new fpecies of culture; and it is there that every private individual is provided, gratis, with fuch plants and feeds as he may have occafion for, together with the

necef-

neceffary inftructions for their cultivation. Thefe gardens furnifh, in the greateft abundance, herbage and fruits of various kinds to the company's fhips.

Travellers cannot but with pleafure and admiration obferve large enclofures confecrated to the ftudy and improvement of botany, in which the moft rare and ufeful plants, from every quarter of the world, are arranged in the moft excellent order: the curious have the additional fatiffaction alfo of finding fkilful gardeners, who take pleafure in defcribing and pointing out their virtues.

Thofe beautiful gardens are terminated by large orchards, where are to be found all the fruits of Europe, together with feveral natives of

Africa

Africa and Afia. Nothing is more agreeable than to fee in different expofitions, even in the fame enclofure, the chefnut, the apple, and other trees, from the moft northern climates, together with the mufcadine of the Indies, the camphres of Borneo, the palms, and a variety of other trees, which are natives of the torrid zone.

MADAGASCAR.

After doubling the Cape of Good Hope, you enter the Indian fea, where you find the great ifland of Madagafcar: we are ftill unacquainted with many places of this ifland, though the Portuguefe, Dutch, French, and other Europeans have had fettlements, and frequented it above two centuries. Thofe parts, which

which we know, are very fertile, and the inhabitants would, in all probability, cultivate them extremely well, were there a vent for their productions. They rear numerous herds of cattle and sheep; their pasturages, such as nature has formed them, are rich: in many cantons are large tracts of tilled ground, covered with grass of an extraordinary size, which grows to the height of five or six feet; the natives call it *Fatak*; it is excellent for nourishing and fattening their horned cattle, which are of the largest species, and differ in shape from ours, particularly by a large fleshy protuberance on their neck. — Another grass, of a finer blade, shoots spontaneously through the sands on the sea coast, which furnishes food for the sheep: these are of the same species with those of Barbary, and differ

from

from ours moſt remarkably, by the monſtrous ſize of their tails, which weigh in general from ſix to eight pounds.

The Madecaſſes or Malegaches (which is the name of the inhabitants of this iſland) cultivate ſcarce any other grain but rice : they ſow at the commencement of the rainy ſeaſon ; in conſequence of which they are not under the neceſſity of watering their fields. In labouring their ground, they uſe no other inſtrument but the pick-axe ; they begin by grubbing up all the weeds ; then five or ſix men, ranging themſelves in a line on the field, dig little holes as they paſs along, into which the women or children, who follow, throw the grains of the rice, and then with their feet cover them with earth : a field

field fown in this manner, produces an increafe of above eighty or a hundred-fold, which proves rather the extreme fertility of the foil, than the goodnefs of the cultivation: badly underftood as it may be, however, the inhabitants of Madegafcar live in abundance. In no country in the world, that I have feen, are rice and other effential provifions cheaper than in this ifland. For a remnant of coarfe blue cloth, which may be worth perhaps twenty pence, the Madecaffe gives two or three meafures of rice. Thefe meafures are furnifhed by the Europeans, who never fail to enlarge them every year; yet the iflanders do not complain. The meafure is firft of all heaped; the buyer then, in virtue of an eftablifhed right for fecuring good meafure, thrufts his arm to the elbow in the

rice,

rice, and with one sweep empties it almost entirely, which the Madecasse has the patience a second time to replenish, without a murmur. This measure is called a *Gamelle*, which, thus filled, will hold about 160 pounds of pure rice.

There cannot be a doubt, but if our [the French] India Company, who alone are in possession of the trade with the natives of this island, would give proper encouragement to agriculture, it would in a short time make a rapid progress.—Our islands of Bourbon and France would here always find a certain resource against those dearths which too frequently distress the latter of these islands. Our squadrons bound for India, who put into the Isle of France for refreshments, would there always find abundance

dance of provifions brought from Madagafcar, and of confequence would not be fubjected to the neceffity of lofing their time at the Cape, or at Batavia, begging refrefhments from the Dutch, whilft the enemies of France, as happened in the late war, are conquering their fettlements, and deftroying their trade.*

Wheat would grow in Madagafcar in the fame abundance as rice : it was formerly cultivated fuccefsfully in the fettlement which we then poffeffed at the fouthern point of the ifland, called Fort Dauphin. Even at this day fine ftalks of wheat are ftill to be found there, produced from

---

* Perhaps it may be owing to fome hint here given, that the French (as is reported) are now again endeavouring to eftablifh fettlements on the ifland of Madagafcar.

from the scattered grains of the ancient crops, which being blown about by the winds, have annually, since our being drove from that settlement, sown of themselves, and sprung up at random, amongst the native herbs of the country. The lands there are of inconceivable fertility; the islanders intelligent and ingenious. In those districts where the Arabs have not penetrated, the simple laws of nature are their guides; their manners the manners of the primitive ages. These laws, and these manners, are more favourable for agriculture, than all our sublime speculations, than all our most applauded theories on the most approved practice; than all those ineffectual means now employed to re-animate an art, which our manners teach us to regard with contempt,

or

or treat with levity; and which is perpetually haraſſed, perpetually oppreſſed by innumerable abuſes, which derive their ſource from the very laws themſelves.

THE ISLE OF BOURBON.

Almoſt 200 leagues eaſt of Madagaſcar lie the two iſlands of Bourbon and France; the ſoil of which is naturally as fertile as that of Madagaſcar, whilſt they enjoy a happier climate. Bourbon has no port: it is of conſequence little frequented by the ſhipping. The inhabitants have preſerved their ſimplicity of manners, and agriculture is there in a flouriſhing ſtate. The iſland produces wheat, rice, and maize, not only for its own conſumpt, but even furniſhes a ſmall ſupply to the Iſle of France:

France: the culture there is the fame as at Madagafcar. The horned cattle and fheep, which they have imported from that ifland, thrive here extremely well, efpecially as they have alfo introduced the grafs called *Fatak*, which, as I have before obferved, makes excellent pafturage.

The lands of this ifland are principally employed in the culture of the coffee-tree. The firft plants of this fhrubby tree were brought from Mocha. It multiplies by its grains, fowing fpontaneoufly; little attention is required; nothing more is neceffary than to grub up, three or four times during the firft year, the neighbouring weeds, which would otherwife rob it of its proper nourifhment: the fecond year it grows without care; its branches which extend hori-

horizontally along the furface of the ground, by their fhade ftifle the growth of all fuch weeds, as might fhoot up within their circumference: at the end of eighteen months the coffee-tree begins to bear fruit, and in three years yields a plentiful crop. They plant thefe trees chequer-wife, at about the diftance of feven feet from one another, and, when they grow too tall, prune them to the height of perhaps two feet from the ground.

The coffee-tree demands a light foil: it thrives better in fand almoft pure, than in rich ground: they obferve in the ifle of Bourbon, that thefe trees yield annually, one with another about a pound of coffee: this fruit comes to perfection, and is gathered-in during dry weather, which gives it a great advantage over the Weſt India coffee, which never ripens nor is got-in but in the rainy ſeaſons. The coffee, after it is gathered-in, muſt be dried; for ſeveral days, therefore, it is expoſed to the ſun, till the bean becomes extremely dry; they then clear it of the pulp, which is done by peſtles in large wooden troughs.

THE ISLE OF FRANCE.

This iſland poſſeſſes two excellent harbours, where all the ſhipping of the French Company, employed in the commerce of China and the Indies, touch for refreſhments; here alſo rendezvous their armaments in times of war: this iſland is, of conſequence, not ſo ſolitary as Bourbon. The politics and manners of Europe have

have here more influence. The lands are as fertile as thofe of Bourbon; rivulets, which are never dry, water it like a garden: notwithftanding which the harvefts often fail, and fcarcity is here almoft perpetually felt.

Since the days of the celebrated M. de la Bourdonnois (who governed this ifland for ten or twelve years, and ought to be regarded as the founder of the colony, for his introduction and patronage of agriculture) they have wandered inceffantly from project to project; attempting the culture of almoft every fpecies of plants, without properly profecuting any one of them. The coffee, the cotton, the indigo, the fugar-cane, the pear, the cinnamon, the mulberry, the tea, and the cocoa trees, have all been cultivated by experiments, but in fuch a fuperficial manner as could never fecure fuccefs. Had they followed the fimple plan of the founder which was to fecure bread, the ifland would at this day have been flourifhing; abundance would then have reigned amongft the colonifts, and the fhipping never been difappointed of the neceffary refrefhments and provifions.

The cultivation of grain, neverthelefs, though neglected and badly underftood, is that which fucceeds the beft. Thofe lands, which are fo employed, yield annually a crop of wheat, and another of rice or Turkey corn, without the intervention of one fallow year, and without the leaft improvement, or
any

any other mode of labour, than that which is practifed at Madagafcar.

The *Maniac* was firſt introduced into this iſland by M. de la Bourdonnois: the culture of this plant was at firſt attended with very great difficulty, but is now the principal refource of the coloniſts for the nouriſhment of their ſlaves. As the culture of this root is here the fame as in America, I ſhall not repeat what has been related by a number of travellers.

They formerly brought from Madagafcar black cattle and ſheep; but fince they have difcovered that more advantage attends the tranfportation of ſlaves, they have neglected the increafe of their cattle, which the continual demands of the ſhipping, and the wants of the inhabitants at the fame time, daily diminifh: befides, they have never hitherto formed any paftures; fuch as they have attempted having been laid out with fo little fkill, that they have not fucceeded. The ifland produces naturally, in different cantons, an excellent kind of grafs, which grows to the heighth of five or fix feet. This grafs begins to appear above ground about the beginning of the rainy feafon; it performs all its vegetation during the three months, which this feafon lafts: the inhabitants take advantage of this to pafture their herds, who fatten upon it amazingly; but, the vegetation over, there remains nothing on the ground but a ftraw too hard to afford nourifhment to the cattle; and, foon after, the fire, which is kindled here by a thoufand

acci-

accidents, confumes this ftraw, and with it frequently part of the neighbouring forefts. During the remainder of the year, the herds wander about and languifh amongft the woods.

The greateft fault which has been committed in this ifland, and which has proved moft prejudicial to cultivation, is the method of clearing the woods from off the grounds by fire, without leaving groves and thickets at proper diftances. The rains, in this ifland, conduce moft to the amelioration of the grounds; but the clouds being ftopt by the forefts, there the rains fall; whilft the cleared lands are fcarce watered by a fingle drop: the fields, at the fame time, being thus deprived of defence, are expofed to the violence of the winds,

which

which often entirely deftroy the harvefts.—The Dutch, as we have before obferved, found no trees at the Cape; but they have planted them there, as fhelter for their habitations. The Ifle of France, on the contrary, was covered with woods, and the colonifts have entirely deftroyed them.

COAST OF COROMANDEL.

Agriculture has ever flourifhed in the Eaft-Indies; it has, however, degenerated fince the conqueft of this country by the Moguls; who, like all barbarous nations, have defpifed that induftry which nourifhes mankind, to attach themfelves to that deftructive art which defolates the earth.

The

The conquerors, when they took poffeflion of the country, appropriated to themfelves at the fame time all the lands. The Mogul emperors divided them into great moveable fiefs, which they diftributed amongft their grandees; thefe farmed them out to their vaffals; and thofe again to others; fo that the lands are now no longer cultivated but by the fervants and day-labourers of the fub-farmers.

As no country in the world is more expofed to revolution than the Indies, fubjected to mafters whofe government is an abfolute anarchy, the poffeffor of the fief, as well as the farmer, for ever uncertain of their fate endeavour to make the moft of the lands and their cultivators, without ever beftowing a thought on improvement.

provement. Fortunately for thefe Barbarian conquerors, the conquered natives, inviolably attached to their ancient manners, apply themfelves inceffantly to agriculture, from inclination, and from religion. Notwithftanding the frantic defpotifm of the Mogul government, the Malabar *, defpifing and pitying the mafter whom he obeys, cultivates, with the fame ardor as if he was proprietor, the fields of his anceftors, the care of which is confided to him by the ufurper.

The labourers are a tribe much honoured among the Indians. Religion has confecrated agriculture, even to

* The French give the name of Malabar, not only to the ancient inhabitants of the Malabar coaft, but in general to the Aborigines of the great Peninfula of Indoftan.

to the animals deftined for the labour of the ground. As the Indies in general are deficient in paftures, as horfes are fcarce, as buffaloes and other cattle for the draught multiply but flowly, the ancient Indian policy made it a crime againft their religion to kill thefe ufeful animals.——The Malabars make them more ferviceable than any other people: they employ them, as we do, in labouring the ground; as alfo in drawing their carriages, and in carrying every kind of load: there are no other beafts of burden in the neighbourhood of Pondicherry. I am convinced that in every country they might be rendered equally ufeful.

The foil on the Coromandel coaft is light, dry, and fandy; the induftry and labour, however, of the natives

tives make it produce two crops every year, without the neceſſity of one fallow ſeaſon. After the rice harveſt is over, there is always a crop of ſome ſmaller grains, ſuch as millet, and a ſpecies of French beans, of which India produces a variety of different kinds.

The moſt remarkable proceſs of Indian huſbandry, is the watering their grounds for the culture of rice.

MACHINE FOR WATERING RICE-GROUNDS.

If the grounds they propoſe watering, have neither rivulet nor fountain ſufficiently abundant, they dig a pit-well, on the brink of which they raiſe a pillar of near the ſame height as the depth of the well. At the

the fummit of this pillar, which is forked, is an iron bar, which crofling both divifions horizontally, fupports a kind of fee-faw, to one end of which a ladder is fufpended; the other end of this fee-faw projects from the top of the pillar about three feet, having a long pole faftened to it in a pofition parallel with the pillar, at which hangs a large bucket of wood or copper: by the fide of this machine is a large refervoir, built with bricks and clofely cemented, elevated above the level of the grounds they propofe to water; the opening whence the waters are difcharged being on that fide which fronts the field. Every thing being thus difpofed, a man afcends to the top of the column, by the ladder fixed to the fee-faw: as foon as he has reached the top, another man,

ftationed

ſtationed by the ſide of the reſervoir, plunges the bucket, which is ſuſpended by the pole, into the well; upon which he at the top deſcends the ladder, and bringing thereby the bucket full of water to a level with the reſervoir, the other there empties it. As ſoon as the reſervoir is full, they open a kind of ſluice; the inundation begins, and is kept conſtantly flowing by the operations of theſe two men, who ſometimes are thus employed whole days, the one aſcending and deſcending, the other throwing the bucket into the well, and emptying it when full.

MODE OF LABOUR.

The Malabars labour their grounds with inſtruments reſembling the Aire and the Souchée, in uſe in the ſouth

of

of France. They employ oxen, but more commonly buffaloes; thefe laſt being ſtronger, and more capable of enduring the heat, than the oxen, which on the coaſt of Coromandel, are generally weakly, and of a ſmall ſize.

FLOCKS OF SHEEP, &c.

Thefe animals are generally fed with the ſtraw of rice, ſome herbs, and boiled beans. Here and there in the fields you fee ſome ſmall flocks of goats, and others of ſheep, which differ from ours by their being covered with hair inſtead of wool. They are known in the French colonies by the name of *Chiens marous*. Thefe flocks, however, are lean, and multiply but ſlowly.

Were

Were the inhabitants of India to eat the flesh of animals, like the Europeans, their cattle would very soon be destroyed. It appears, therefore, that the religious law rendering it criminal for an Indian to eat the flesh of animals, has been dictated by the wisdom of sound policy, which has employed the authority of religion to secure obedience to a regulation which the nature of the climate required.

The principal food of the Malabars is grain, butter, pulse, and fruits. They eat nothing which has ever enjoyed life. The countries to the south and west of Indostan, are the granaries of this vast continent, and maintain the inhabitants in abundance. These countries still remain

in

in the poffeflion of the Aborigines of the country, whofe laws are extremely favourable for agriculture. The Moguls have endeavoured often to make themfelves mafters of thefe countries, but hitherto in vain.

GARDENS.

In the Malabar gardens there is no kind of pulfe equal to ours. Exclufive of the various kinds of Frenchbean, fome of which are of the arborefcent kind; the beft they cultivate is the *Bazella*, known in France by the name of the *Spinage of China*; this is a lively, clambering plant, which, while growing, they fupport upon fticks, like our peafe, or prop up againft the walls, which it very foon covers with a moft agreeable verdure

verdure; its taſte is almoſt the ſame with our ſpinage.

Gardening is but little known on the Coromandel coaſt. The orchards are better ſupplied than the gardens; yet they have no fruits that can be compared to thoſe of Europe. They do not underſtand the art of engrafting. Their moſt common fruits are the pine-apple, the mango, the bonana, and the gouyave. The two firſt of theſe fruits are but indifferent on the Coromandel coaſt, though excellent on the Malabar coaſt, and ſeveral other parts of India.

THE COCOA-TREE.

The moſt uſeful of all the trees in their orchards is undoubtedly the cocoa-tree. This tree bears cluſters of

nuts

nuts of an immenſe ſize. When theſe nuts are ripe, they yield a ſpecies of oil in great abundance, which the Indians uſe for various purpoſes, particularly in ſeaſoning their garden ſtuff; the taſte of this oil, however, is extremely diſagreeable to thoſe who are not accuſtomed to eat it. But the method of rendering the culture of this tree moſt advantageous, is the extracting wine from its fruit. The Indian watches the time when the nuts of the cocoa-tree have attained to the ſize of our ordinary nuts, which happens ſoon after the fall of the flower: he then makes an inciſion in the ſtalk of the cluſter about ſeven or eight inches from the trunk of the tree; here he faſtens an earthen veſſel to receive the juice, which iſſues in great abundance: the mouth of the veſſel he carefully

wraps

wraps round with a cloth, to prevent the admiſſion of the air, which would ſoon turn it to the fret. The veſſel fills in twenty-four hours: the Indian takes care to change it every day. This natural wine which is called *Soury*, is ſold and drunk in this ſtate. It has much of the taſte and ſtrength of the *Muſt*, or new wine of the grape: it keeps, however, but a few days; it is neceſſary then to diſtil it, otherwiſe it would ſour, and become entirely uſeleſs. This ſpecies of wine, when diſtilled, is the well-known liquor called *Arrack*.

A cocoa-tree, thus managed, is worth a pagoda (about eight ſhillings) per annum. Theſe trees are planted about twenty-five or thirty feet diſtant from each other. They

produce

produce nothing for ten or twelve years, but then annually bear fruit for above fifty years. They flourish beft in a mixed fandy foil; and fucceed extremely well even in pure fand.

The Malabars cultivate, in the open fields, a variety of plants, whofe productions are of an oily fubftance; fuch as the *Sefame* or *Gergelin*, which is a kind of fox-grafs, and the *Ricin* or *Palma Chrifti*. The frefh oil extracted from this plant, which is known in Europe for a violent and dangerous cauftic, cannot have the fame hurtful quality in the Indies, as the Malabars confider it as a gentle purgative, and the beft remedy for almoft all the difeafes incident to infants at the breaft; giving them ufually, every month, a fpoonful of it, mixed

mixed in an equal quantity of their mother's milk.

I ſhall conclude this article by obſerving, that the reader muſt not form an idea of agriculture over the Indies in general, from the ſketch I have given of that on the Coromandel coaſt : this coaſt, and the countries adjacent, form but a ſmall part of the Eaſt-Indies, properly ſo called : they are, at the ſame time, the moſt barren, and have ſuffered moſt from the devaſtations of the Moguls, from the deſtructive government of theſe conquerors, and from the continual wars which harraſs and depopulate the country. The coaſts of Orixa, Malabar, the territory of Surat, the banks of the Ganges, and the interior parts of Indoſtan, are much more fertile, and in many of theſe
coun-

countries agriculture flourishes surprisingly.—I relate nothing but facts, which I had opportunities of observing myself.

THE KINGDOM OF SIAM.

The kingdom of Siam, situate on the peninsula of the Indies beyond the Ganges, is in general extremely fertile. Divided, like Indostan, by a chain of mountains from north to south, it enjoys, all the year round, and at the same time, two very opposite seasons. The western division, all along the bay of Bengal, is deluged by continual rains, during the six months that the monsoons continue to blow from the west. This season is considered as their winter on this coast; whilst in the other division of the kingdom, towards the east, they

enjoy

enjoy the fineſt climate, and never experience that difference of feaſon, which reigns on the weſtern ſide, except by the overflowing of the Menam. This noble river runs along a great way among mountains, where the rains concenter : it waſhes the walls of the capital, and annually overflows, without the leaſt ravage, a delightful country, covered all over with rice plantations. The ſlime, which the Menam leaves behind, enriches the ſoil prodigiouſly ; the rice ſeems to grow up in proportion as the inundation riſes, and the river at length gently retires by degrees into its bed, as the rice approaches to maturity, and has no further occaſion for its waters. How bountiful has nature been to thoſe who inhabit this charming country!—ſhe has, however, done more : the fields pro-

produce, in profusion, an infinite variety of moſt delicate fruits, which require almoſt no cultivation; ſuch as the pine-apple, the mangouſtas, (the moſt delicate fruit perhaps in the world) mangoes of different kinds, and all excellent, ſeveral ſpecies of oranges, the banana, the ducion, the gacca, with other fruits of an inferior quality. Nature, ſtill more bountiful, has alſo ſcattered over this country, almoſt on the ſurface of the ground, mines of gold, copper, and a ſpecies of fine tin, which there, as in other parts of India, they name *Calin*.

In this terreſtrial paradiſe, ſurrounded with ſo much riches, who would imagine that the Siameſe are, perhaps, the moſt wrethed people in the world?

The government of Siam is despotic: the sovereign alone enjoys that liberty which is natural to all mankind: his subjects are all his slaves; every one of them is annually taxed at six months personal service without wages, and even without food: he allows them the other six months to procure themselves wherewithal to exist the year. Under such a government, there is no law that can afford protection to individuals against violence, or in the smallest degree secure them in their property. Every thing is subjected to the caprice of a prince, rendered brutal by every species of excess, particularly that of power; who passes his days locked up in his seraglio, without an idea of any thing beyond the walls of his palace; and particularly ignorant of

the

the wretched condition of his subjects. Thefe are expofed to the avarice of the grandees, who themfelves are only the chief flaves, and tremblingly approach, on appointed days, the prefence of their tyrant, whom they adore like a divinity, though fubject to the moft dangerous caprices.

Religion alone has preferved the power of protecting againft tyranny thofe who, ranging themfelves under its ftandard, are admitted into the order of the priefts of *Somonacondom*, the deity of the Siamefe. Thofe who embrace this order, and their number is confiderable, are by law obliged to obferve the ftricteft celibacy, which, in a warm climate, fuch as that of Siam, whilft it occafions

great

great diforders, almoft depopulates the country.

It may eafily be conceived, that under fuch a government agriculture cannot flourifh; it may be faid, even, that no regard is paid to it at all, when the fmall portion of ground which is laboured, is compared to the immenfe extent of lands which are totally neglected.

With regard even to thofe grounds which they have laid out, nature may be faid to do every thing. Men oppreffed, debafed, without fpirit, nay, in a manner without hands, give themfelves fcarce any other trouble than juft to reap what the earth produces; and, as the country is extenfive, and thinly peopled, they enjoy

enjoy abundance of neceffaries, almoft without labour.

From the port of Mergin, fituated on the weftern coaft of this kingdom, to the capital, during a journey of ten or twelve days, you crofs immenfe plains, charmingly watered, and the foil excellent: fome of which appear to have been formerly tilled, but now lie quite uncultivated. This journey travellers are under the neceflity of making in caravans, in order to defend themfelves from the tygers and the elephants, to which this fine country is in a manner entirely abandoned, during a journey of eight days there fcarce being the veftige of a habitation.

The environs of the capital are cultivated; the lands belonging to the king,

king, those of the princes, the ministers, and principal officers display the amazing fertility of the country, producing, as I have been assured, an increase of two hundred-fold.

The Siamese method of cultivating their rice, is first to sow it very thick in a small square plot of ground, well watered, a little below the surface of the earth. As soon as the plants have grown about five or six inches high, they pull them up by the roots, and transplant them in small parcels of three or four stalks, distant from each other about four inches every way. These plants are placed deep in a clay soil, which has been previously well laboured with a plow, drawn by two buffaloes. The rice, transplanted in this manner, has beyond comparison a much greater

in-

increase, than if allowed to grow up in the same ground where it was originally planted.

It is the Chinese, and the Cochinchinese, settled in the capital and its neighbourhood, who contribute most to the improvement of the grounds. These strangers are useful to the sovereign, by the commerce they carry on with him, and it is the interest of the government to protect them from oppression.

In the neighbourhood of the uncultivated lands I have mentioned, you find others, belonging to different individuals, who, discouraged by continual oppressions, have quite abandoned them. It is astonishing, however, to observe these lands, frequently neither laboured nor sown

for

for years together, produce extraordinary crops of rice. The grain, reaped negligently, sows of itself, and re-produces annually another harvest, by the help of the inundations of the river Menam; which proves, at the same time, the extreme fertility of the ground, and the extreme misery of the inhabitants.

The orchards of the prince, and the great Talapoins *, are admirable for the variety of their fruits, all of the most exquisite kind; but these delicacies no private individual is allowed to enjoy. When a man is so unhappy as to have in his grounds a tree of excellent fruit, such as the mangoustas, a party of soldiers never fail to come every year, to secure, for the

* A religious order.

the king, or some great minister, the produce of this tree. They take an account of every mangousta, good or bad, making the proprietor guardian and security for the whole; and, when the fruits ripen, should there happen the smallest deficiency, the poor proprietor is subjected to all the insolence of unrestrained power; it becomes, of consequence, a real misfortune for a private man to be possessed of such a tree.

The Siamese rear herds of buffaloes, and horned cattle; but all the care they take of them is, to conduct them, in the day time, to the fallow grounds, which abound in pastures, and re-conduct them, in the evening, to the inclosures, in order to secure them from the tygers, of which there are great numbers in this country.

The

The milk, and a very little labour, is all the advantage they draw from them. Their religion, which is the fame that prevails in Indoſtan, and which the Talapoins alone know any thing about, forbids them killing theſe animals. They elude, however, this law, by ſelling them to the Mahometans ſettled among them, who kill them, and ſell their fleſh privately. They have alſo great numbers of poultry, particularly ducks, of the beſt kinds in the Indies.

The king maintains a number of tame elephants. Each of theſe monſtrous animals has twelve or fifteen men daily employed in cutting herbs, bananiers, (a kind of large roſe) and ſugar-canes. They are after all of no real uſe; they ſerve only for ſhew. They diſplay, ſay the Siameſe, amefe, the grandeur of their prince; and he conceives an idea of his greatnefs, more from the number of his elephants, than from the number of his fubjects.

Thefe animals, wherever they come, make moft deftructive havock; of this their keepers take advantage, making every individual, who is poffeffed of cultivated lands, or gardens, pay annually a certain tribute: fhould they refufe, the elephants would immediately be let loofe, and ravage and ruin defolate their fields: for what fubject would be hardy enough to dare to fail in refpect to the elephants of the king of Siam, many of which, to the difgrace of humanity, are loaded with a profufion of titles, and preferred to the firft dignities in the kingdom.

THE MALAIS.

Beyond the kingdom of Siam is the peninfula of Malacca; a country formerly well peopled, and, confequently, well cultivated. This nation was once one of the greateft powers, and made a very confiderable figure on the theatre of Afia. The fea was covered with their fhips, and they carried on a moft extenfive commerce. Their laws, however, were apparently very different from thofe which fubfift among them at prefent. From time to time they fent out numbers of colonies, which, one after another, peopled the iflands of Sumatra, Java, Borneo, the Celebes or Macaffor, the Moluccas, the Philippines, and thofe innumerable iflands of the Archipelago, which bound Afia on the eaft, and which occupy

cupy an extent of feven hundred leagues in longitude, from eaft to weft, by about fix hundred of latitude, from north to fouth. The inhabitants of all thefe iflands, thofe at leaft upon the coafts, are the fame people; they fpeak almoft the fame language, have the fame laws, the fame manners. — Is it not fomewhat fingular, that this nation, whofe poffeffions are fo extenfive, fhould fcarce be known in Europe?—I fhall endeavour to give you an idea of thofe laws, and thofe manners; you will, from thence, eafily judge of their agriculture.

Travellers, who make obfervations on the Malais, are aftonifhed to find, in the center of Afia, under the fcorching climate of the line, the laws, the manners, the cuftoms, and
the

the prejudices of the ancient inhabitants of the north of Europe. The Malais are governed by feudal laws, that capricious fyftem, conceived for the defence of the liberty of a few, againſt the tyranny of one, whilſt the multitude is ſubjected to ſlavery and oppreſſion.

A chief, who has the title of king, or ſultan, iſſues his commands to his great vaſſals, who obey when they think proper. Theſe have inferior vaſſals, who often act in the ſame manner with regard to them. A ſmall part of the nation live independent, under the title of *Oramfai*, or *noble*, and ſell their ſervices to thoſe who pay them beſt; whilſt the body of the nation is compoſed of ſlaves, and live in perpetual ſervitude.

With

With thefe laws the Malais are reftlefs, fond of navigation, war, plunder, emigrations, colonies, defperate enterprizes, adventures, and gallantry. They talk inceffantly of their honour, and their bravery, whilft they are univerfally confidered, by thofe with whom they have intercoufe, as the moft treacherous, ferocious people on the face of the globe; and yet, 'which appeared to me extremely fingular, they fpeak the fofteft language of Afia. That which the Count de Forbin has faid, in his memoirs, of the ferocity of the Macaffars, is exactly true, and is the reigning characteriftic of the whole Malay nations. More attached to the abfurd laws of their pretended honour, than to thofe of juftice or humanity, you always obferve, that

amongft

amongst them, the strong oppress and destroy the weak: their treaties of peace and friendship never subsisting beyond that self-interest which induced them to make them, they are almost always armed, and either at war amongst themselves, or employed in pillaging their neighbours.

This ferocity, which the Malais qualify under the name of courage, is so well known to the European companies, who have settlements in the Indies, that they have universally agreed in prohibiting the captains of their ships, who may put into the Malay islands, from taking on board any seamen of that nation, except in the greatest distress, and then, on no account, to exceed two or three.

It

It is nothing uncommon for a handful of thefe horrid favages fuddenly to embark, attack a veffel by furprize, poignard in hand, maffacre the people, and make themfelves mafters of her. Malay batteaus, with twenty-five or thirty men, have been known to board European fhips of thirty or forty guns, in order to take poffeffion of them, and murder with their poignards great part of the crew. The Malay hiftory is full of fuch enterprizes, which mark the defperate ferocity of thefe barbarians.

The Malais, who are not flaves, go always armed : they would think themfelves difgraced, if they went abroad without their poignards which they call *Crit*. The induftry of this

this nation even surpasses itself, in the fabrick of this destructive weapon.

As their lives are a perpetual round of agitation and tumult, they could never endure the long flowing habits, which prevail amongst the other Asiatics. The habits of the Malais are exactly adapted to their shapes, and loaded with a multitude of buttons, which fasten them close to their bodies in every part. — I relate these seemingly trifling observations, in order to prove, that, in climates the most opposite, the same laws produce similar manners, customs, and prejudices. Their effect is the same too with respect to agriculture.

The lands possessed by the Malais are, in general, of a superior quality.

lity. Nature feems to have taken pleafure in there affembling her moft favourite productions. They have not only thofe to be found in the territories of Siam, but a variety of others peculiar to thefe iflands. The country is covered with odoriferous woods, fuch as the eagle or aloes wood, the fandal, and the caffia odorata, a fpecies of cinnamon. You there breathe an air impregnated with the odours of innumerable flowers of the greateft fragrance, of which there is a perpetual fucceffion the year round, the fweet flavour of which captivates the foul, and infpires the moft voluptuous fenfations. No traveller, wandering over the plains of Malacca, but feels himfelf ftrongly impelled to wifh his refidence fixed in a place fo luxuriant in allurements,
where

where nature triumphs without the affiftance of art.

The Malay iflands produce various kinds of dying woods, particularly the *Sapan*, which is the fame with the Brafil wood. There are alfo a number of gold mines, which the inhabitants of Sumatra and Malacca call *Ophirs:* fome of which, thofe efpecially on the eaftern coaft, are richer than thofe of Brazil or Peru. There are likewife mines of fine copper, mixed with gold, which the inhabitants name *Tombage*. In the iflands of Sumatra and Banea are mines of calin, or fine tin; and at Succadana, in the ifland of Borneo, is a mine of diamonds. Thofe iflands enjoy alfo, exclufively, the rotin, the fagou, (or bread-palm-tree) the camphre, and other precious aromatics,

matics, which we know under the names of various spiceries.

The sea too teems with abundance of excellent fish, together with ambergris, pearls, and those delicate birds nests (so much in request in China) formed in the rocks with the spawn of fishes, and the foam of the sea, by a species of small-sized swallow, peculiar to those seas: this is of such an exquisite substance and flavour, that the Chinese long purchased them for their weight in gold, and still buy them at an excessive price.

In the midst of all this luxuriance of nature, the Malay is miserable. The culture of the lands, abandoned to slaves, is fallen into contempt. These wretched labourers, dragged
incessantly

inceffantly from their ruftic employments, by their reftlefs mafters, who delight in war and maritime enterprizes, have rarely time, and never refolution, to give the neceffary attention to the labouring of their grounds. Their lands, in general, remain uncultivated; and produce no kind of grain for the fubfiftence of the inhabitants.

SAGOU.

The fagou-tree, in part, fupplies the defect of grain. This admirable tree is a prefent which bountiful nature has made to men incapable of labour. It requires no culture; it is a fpecies of the palm-tree, which grows naturally, in the woods, to the height of about twenty or thirty feet; its circumference being fometimes

times from five to six. Its ligneous bark is about an inch in thickneſs, and covers a multitude of long fibres, which, being interwoven one with another, envelope a maſs of a gummy kind of meal. As ſoon as this tree is ripe, a whitiſh duſt, which tranſpires through the pores of the leaves, and adheres to their extremities, proclaims its maturity. The Malais then cut them down near the root, divide them into ſeveral ſections, which they ſplit into quarters: they then ſcoop out the maſs of mealy ſubſtance, which is enveloped by and adheres to the fibres; they dilute it in pure water, and then paſs it through a ſtraining bag of fine cloth, in order to ſeparate it from the fibres. When this paſte has loſt part of its moiſture by evaporation,

poration, the Malais throw it into a kind of earthen veffels, of different fhapes, where they allow it to dry and harden. This pafte is wholefome nourifhing food, and preferves for many years.

The Indians, in general, when they eat the fagou, ufe no other preparation than diluting it in water; but fometimes they drefs it after different manners: they have the art of feparating the fineft of the flour, and reducing it to little grains, fomewhat refembling grains of rice. The fagou, thus prepared, is preferred to the other, for the aged and infirm; and is an excellent remedy for many complaints in the ftomach. When diluted, either in cold or boiling water, it forms a whitifh jelly, very agreeable to the tafte.

Though

Though this fagou-bearing-palm grows naturally in the forests, the Malay chiefs have formed considerable plantations of it, which constitute one of their principal resources for subsistence.

They might have the finest orchards in the world, would they give themselves the trouble to collect the various plants of those excellent fruits which nature has so liberally bestowed upon them: we find, however, none but a few straggling trees planted at random around their houses, or dispersed over their lands without symmetry or order.

The inhabitants of the great island of Java have somewhat better ideas of agriculture, than the other Malais,

since

since their subjection to the government of the Dutch. These sovereign merchants have taken advantage of the feudal system of the Malais, to reduce them under their yoke; artfully weakening the regal power, by fomenting, at times, the rebellions of the great vassals; and humbling the vassals, in their turn, by succouring their princes, when drove to the brink of ruin.

The Javanese begin to recover from that state of anarchy, the consequence of their ancient laws now almost no longer remembered. They cultivate, with success, rice, coffee, indigo, and sugar-cane. They rear, on the eastern coast of the island and in the districts of Madur and Solor, in the neighbourhood, numerous herds of buffa-

loes,

loes, of a monstrous size; their flesh is excellent, and they are of infinite use in labouring the ground. They have likewise numbers of horned cattle, the largest and finest, perhaps, in the world. The common pasturage in this and the rest of the Malay islands, is the same grass I have mentioned under the article of the isle of France, which the colonists there almost entirely neglect.

Here it would be proper to describe the manner of cultivating the spiceries, the indigo, the sugar-cane, and the camphre; but these must be the subject of another discourse. I could have wished also to have comprehended, in this memoir, the observations I have made on the husbandry of China. You could then have compared nation against nation; and,

after

after having observed agriculture despised and debased amongst barbarians, oppressed and loaded with fetters by their frantic laws, the genuine productions of delirium incompatible with reason, you would have beheld this art, (divine it may be called, as taught to man by the great author of his being) supported and protected by the most simple of laws, those of nature, dictated by her to the first inhabitants of the earth, and preserved, since the beginning of time, from generation to generation, by one of the wisest and greatest nations in the world. This comparative representation, whilst, on the one hand, it displayed the misery and misfortunes of every kind, which attend the neglect of agriculture, would, on the other, have demonstrated

ſtrated how much this art, honoured, protected, and encouraged as it ought, will ever advance the happineſs of the human race.

END OF PART FIRST.

TRAVELS

OF A

PHILOSOPHER.

PART SECOND.

TRAVELS

OF A

PHILOSOPHER.

PART SECOND.

I LAST year began to give you a sketch of my inquiries into the state of agriculture among different nations of Africa and Asia. I observed, that scarce a vestige of it could be traced amongst the stupid the indolent negroes, who inhabit the western coasts of Africa; whilst it flourished, under the shade of liberty, amongst the Hollanders at the Cape of Good Hope. I pointed out the happy abundance which reigned

in

in the fertile ifland of Madagafcar, inhabited by a people governed by the greateſt fimplicity of manners, and unacquainted with other laws than thofe of nature. Whilſt I did juſtice alſo to the fyſtem of cultivation that prevailed at the Iſle of Bourbon, which, having no port, and of confequence little or no intercourfe with Europe, the coloniſts have preferved an uncorrupted fyſtem of manners, ever favourable for agriculture, I was, at the fame time, under the neceſſity of acknowledging, that this art, which requires perfeverance and fimplicity, was greatly neglected at the Iſle of France, which, having two excellent ports, and being much frequented by European fhips, was more influenced by the inconſtant and volatile manners of our quarter of the world; and that, in confequence

quence, though the foil, in point of fertility, was equal to Madagafcar and Bourbon, their harvefts generally failed, and an almoft perpetual fcarcity prevailed over the ifland.—I paffed from thence to the great peninfula of the Indies, where agriculture, however oppreffed by the barbarous laws of the Mogul conquerors, is ftill honoured and fupported by the religion, the manners, and the perfeverance of the conquered Malabars. — At Siam, under the happieft climate, and bleffed with a foil inferior in fertility to no country in the world, agriculture we have obferved debafed by the indignities of tyranny, and abandoned by a race of flaves, whom nothing can intereft, after the lofs of liberty.—I have reprefented it almoft in the fame condition

tion amongſt the Malais, who inhabit immenſe dominions, and innumerable iſlands, where nature has diſtributed her choiceſt treaſures, and laviſhed her bounties with a profuſion unknown to other regions. The deſtructive genius of the feudal laws, which keep this people in a perpetual ferment, permits not their application to the culture of the fineſt ſoil in the world. Nature alone does all. I am convinced that if the other nations of the earth, who have the misfortune to be governed by the feudal ſyſtem, inhabited a climate equally happy, and lands equally fertile with thoſe of the Malais, their agriculture would be equally neglected: neceſſity alone could force the plough into their hands.

In my laſt diſcourſe I endeavoured to give you an idea of the moſt intereſting modes of local agriculture which came under my obſervation: my principal object, however, was to enable you to remark, that in every country, in every quarter of the world, the ſtate of agriculture depends entirely on the eſtabliſhed laws, and, conſequently, on the manners, cuſtoms, and prejudices from which theſe laws derived their origin. I now proceed.

THE

THE POWER OF AGRICULTURE.

ORIGIN OF THE KINGDOM OF PONTHIAMAS.

Departing from the peninfula of Malacca, and the iflands of the Malais, towards the north, I fell in with a fmall territory called *Cancar*, but known, on the marine charts, under the name of *Ponthiamas*. Surrounded by the kingdom of Siam, where defpotifm and depopulation go hand in hand, the dominions of Camboya, where no idea of eftablifhed government fubfifts ; and the territories of the Malais, whofe genius, perpetually agitated by their feudal laws, can endure peace neither at home nor abroad : this charming country, about fifty

fifty years ago, was uncultivated, and almoſt deſtitute of inhabitants.

A Chineſe merchant, commander of a veſſel· which he employed in commerce, frequented theſe coaſts. Being a man of that intelligent reflective genius, which ſo characteriſtically marks his nation, he could not, without pain, behold immenſe tracts of ground condemned to ſterility, though naturally more fertile than thoſe which formed the riches of his own country : he formed, therefore, a plan for their improvement. With this view, having firſt of all hired a number of labourers, ſome Chineſe, others from the neighbouring nations, he, with great addreſs, inſinuated himſelf into the favour of the moſt powerful princes, who, for a certain
ſubſidy,

subsidy, assigned him a guard for his protection.

In the course of his voyage to Batavia, and the Philippine islands, he borrowed from the Europeans their most useful discoveries and improvements, particularly the art of fortification and defence: with regard to internal police, he gave the preference to the Chinese. The profits of his commerce soon enabled him to raise ramparts, sink ditches, and provide artillery. These preliminary precautions secured him from a coup de main, and protected him from the enterprizes of the surrounding nations of barbarians.

He distributed the lands to his labourers, without the least reservation of any of those duties or taxes known

by

by the names of fervice or fines of alienation; duties which by allowing no real property, become the moft fatal fcourge to agriculture, and is an idea which revolts againft the common fenfe of every wife nation. He provided his colonifts, at the fame time, with all forts of inftruments proper for the labour and improvement of their grounds.

In forming a labouring and commercial people, he thought, that no laws ought to be framed, but thofe which nature has eftablifhed for the human race in every climate: he made thefe laws refpected by obeying them firft himfelf, and exhibiting an example of fimplicity, induftry, frugality, humanity, and good faith: —— he formed, then, no fyftem of laws—he did more—he eftablifhed morals.

His

His territories foon became the country of every induftrious man, who wifhed to fettle there. His port was open to all nations. The woods were cleared; the grounds judicioufly laboured, and fown with rice; canals, cut from the rivers watered their fields; and plentiful harvefts, after fupplying them with fubfiftence, furnifhed an object of extenfive commerce.

The barbarians of the neighbourhood, amazed to fee abundance fo fuddenly fucceed to fterility, flocked for fubfiftence to the magazines of Ponthiamas; whofe dominions, at this day, are confidered as the moft plentiful granary of that eaftern part of Afia; the Malais, the Cochin-chinefe, the Siamefe, whofe countries are naturally

turally fo fertile, confidering this little territory as the moft certain refource againft famine.

Had the Chinefe founder of this colony of mercantile labourers, in imitation of the fovereigns of Afia, eftablifhed arbitrary impofts; if by the introduction of a feudal fyftem, of which he had examples amongft the neighbouring nations, he had vested in himfelf the fole property of the lands, under the fpecious pretence of giving them away to his colonifts; if he had made luxury reign in his palace, in place of that fimplicity which diftinguifhed his humble dwelling; had he placed his ambition in a brilliant court, and crowds of fawning flaves; had he preferred the agreeable to the ufeful arts, defpifing the induftrious, who labour the ground

with

with the fweat of their brow, and provide fuftenance for themfelves and their fellow creatures ; had he treated his affociates as flaves ; had he received into his port ftrangers in any other fhape than as friends ; his fields had ftill been barren, his dominions unpeopled ; and the wretched inhabitants muft have died of hunger, notwithftanding all their knowledge of agriculture, and all the affiftance they could derive from the moft ufeful inftruments either for tilling or fowing their grounds. But the fage Kiang-tfe, (the name of this judicious Chinefe) perfuaded that he fhould be always rich, if his labourers were fo, eftablifhed only a very moderate duty on all the merchandize entered at his port ; the produce of his lands appearing to him fufficient to render him powerful and great. His integrity,

grity, his moderation, and his humanity made him refpected. He never wifhed to reign; but only to eftablifh the empire of reafon. His fon, who now fills his place, inherits his virtues as well as his poffeffions: by agriculture, and the commerce he carries on with the produce of his lands, he has become fo powerful, that the barbarians, his neighbours, ftile him king, a title which he defpifes. He pretends to no right of fovereignty, but the nobleft of all, that of doing good; happy in being the firft labourer, and the firft merchant of his country, he merits, as well as his father, a title more glorious than that of king—*the friend of mankind.*

How different such men from those conquerors so celebrated, who amaze and desolate the earth; who, abusing the right of conquest, have established laws, which, even after the world has been delivered from these tyrants, has perpetuated, for ages, the miseries of the human race.

CAMBOYA AND TSIAMPA.

To the northward of Ponthiamas we find the countries of Camboya and Tsiampa. They are naturally fertile, (Camboya in particular) and appear, in former times, to have been well cultivated; but the government of these two little states, having no settled form, the inhabitants being perpetually employed in destroying tyrants, only to receive others

others 'in their place, have abandoned the culture of their grounds. Their fields which might be covered with rice, with herds, and with flocks, are deferts; and the natives are reduced to feed on a few wretched roots, which they gather from amidft the brambles, which overfpread their lands.

Travellers are furprifed to find, at a little diftance from the wretched canton of Camboya, the ruins of an old city, built with ftone, the architecture of which has fome refemblance to that of Europe. The neighbouring fields too ftill preferve the traces of ridges: every thing fhews that agriculture and the other arts have once flourifhed there; but they have now difappeared, with the nation who cultivated them. Thofe who at present inhabit this country have no history, no tradition even, which can throw the faintest light upon the subject.

COCHIN-CHINA.

The Cochin-chinese, who border on Camboya to the north, observing the lands of this kingdom desolate and abandoned, some years ago took possession of such tracks as were most convenient, and have there introduced an excellent culture. The province of Donnay, usurped in this manner from Camboya, is at present the granary of Cochin-china. This kingdom, one of the greatest in Eastern Asia, about one hundred and fifty years ago, was inhabited by an inconsiderable nation, barbarous and savage, known by the name of *Loi*,

who,

who, living partly by fishing, partly on roots, and the wild fruits of the country, paid little regard to agriculture.

A Tonquinese prince, unsuccefsful in a war he carried on against the king of Tonquin, (under whom he enjoyed an office somewhat resembling the maires de palais, under the Merovingian race of the kings of France) retired with his soldiers and adherents acrofs the river which divides that kingdom from Cochinchina. The savages, who then poffeffed this country, fled before these strangers, and took refuge among the mountains of Tsiampa. After a long war with their old enemies, who purfued them, the Torquinese fugitives remained at length peaceable poffeffors of the country known under

der the name of Cochin-china: it extends about two hundred leagues from north to south, but narrow and unequal from east to west. They then applied themselves entirely to the cultivation of rice, which, being the ordinary food of the inhabitants of Asia, is to them an object of the greatest importance. They separated into little cantonments, and established themselves on the plains, which extend along the banks of the rivers.

The fertility of the soil, which had lain long uncultivated, soon recompensed their labours by abundance; population increased in proportion to the culture; and their cantons extended in such a manner, that all the plains of this vast country being put into a state of improvement, they were tempted to make encroachments

ments on thofe of Camboya, which were in a manner totally abandoned. I never faw any country where the progrefs of population was fo remarkable as in Cochin-china, which muft be attributed not only to the climate, and the fertility of the foil, but to the fimplicity of their manners, to the prudence and induftry of the women as well as the men, and to the variety of excellent fifh, which, with rice, is their ordinary food.

CULTURE OF DIFFERENT KINDS OF RICE IN COCHIN-CHINA.

The Cochin-chinefe cultivate fix different kinds of rice: the *Little Rice*, the grain of which is fmall, oblong and tranfparent; this is by far the moft delicate; it is generally administred ministered to the sick; the *Great Long Rice* is that whose form is round: the *Red Rice*, so called, because the grain is envellopped in a husk of a reddish colour, which adheres so closely, that it requires a very uncommon operation to separate it. These three kinds are produced in the greatest abundance, and form the principal subsistence of the natives. They require water, it being necessary to overflow the grounds where they are cultivated.

They raise also two other sorts of dry rice, which grow in dry soils, and, like our wheat, require no other watering but what they receive from the clouds. One of these species of rice has a grain as white as snow; when dressed it is of a slimy viscous substance; they make of it different
kinds

kinds of paſte, ſuch as vermicelli. Both theſe kinds form a conſiderable article in their commerce to China. They cultivate them only on the mountains and riſing grounds, which they labour with the ſpade. They ſow theſe grains as we do wheat, about the end of December or beginning of January, when the rainy ſeaſon ends; they are not above three months in the ground, and yield a plentiful crop.

I am induced to believe, that the culture of this valuable grain would ſucceed extremely well in France. In the years 1749 and 1750 I often travelled over the mountains of Cochin-china, where this rice is cultivated; they are very high, and the temperature of the air cold: in the month of January, 1750, I obſerved that

that the rice was very green, and above three inches high, although the liquor in Reaumur's thermometer was only about four degrees above the freezing point.

I carried some quintals of this grain to the Isle of France, where it was sown with success, and produced a greater crop than any other species. The colonists received my present with the greatest eagerness, as, exclusive of its superior increase, it has a finer taste, is attended with less trouble, there being no necessity for overflowing the fields; and, as it ripens fifteen or twenty days sooner than the other kinds, it can be reaped and secured before the hurricane season, which frequently makes dreadful havock with their later harvests. The other kinds of rice, being of a

slower

flower growth, require their grounds to be laid under water, after the manner of the natives of the Coromandel coaſt *; but our coloniſts pay ſo little attention to agriculture, that they have never hitherto introduced it.

One might have imagined, that the advantages flowing from the cultivation of dry rice, would have engaged the coloniſts to attend to it with the greateſt care; and that, from the Iſle of France, it might have been with eaſe introduced into Europe: but I have in vain endeavoured to procure it from this iſland; thoſe to whom I have applied, have ſent me only common rice, which demands water and warmth. The culture of dry rice has,

* See page 39.

has, like every other species of agriculture, been abandoned to the unexperienced ignorance of slaves, who have mixed all the different kinds together, in such a manner, that the rice of Cochin-china being ripe long before the others, the grains have dropt from the ears before they were reaped, and the species, in this manner, has been, by degrees, entirely lost in that island. Would any traveller, whom business or curiosity might lead to Cochin-china, send over but a few pounds of this excellent grain, he would deserve our warmest acknowledgments.

The Cochin-chinese cultivate the common rice nearly in the same manner with the Malabars on the Coromandel coast. After having twice ploughed their ground, they sow

the

the rice in a little field which has been well laboured with the spade; the surface of this little field they just cover with water, to the height only of a few lines; and as soon as the rice is about five or six inches high, they harrow over their large fields, and overflow them with water; then pulling up the rice-plants in the seed-plots, transplant them into these grounds, thus prepared, in small parcels of four or five stalks, about the distance of six inches the one from the other. Women and children are generally employed in this work.

The Cochin-chinese have no machine for overflowing their grounds, nor have they any occasion: their plains, from one end of the kingdom to the other, are commanded by

a chain

a chain of high mountains, plentifully fupplied with fprings and rivulets, which naturally overflow the grounds, according as their courfe is directed.

They cultivate likewife different kinds of grains, fuch as the mahis, millets of different forts, feveral fpecies of the French bean, potatoes, yams, and a variety of roots proper for the fubfiftence of men and animals. But the culture of moft important advantage to them, next to the rice, is the fugar-cane; and no country in Afia produces it in greater abundance than the Cochin-china.

SUGAR-CANES.

The fugar-canes of this country are of two kinds: the firft grows thick and tall, the joints at a confiderable diftance

diftance from one another, the colour always green, the juice abundant, with very little of the falt in it. This fpecies of cane is in general ufe for feeding and fattening of cattle; and experience teaches them, that no kind of food fattens fooner or better the human fpecies, as well as animals, than this fugar-cane, eat while green, and the fugar which is extracted from it.

The fecond fpecies is fmaller in every refpect, with its joints approaching nearer together: when ripe it affumes a yellow colour; and contains lefs water, and more falt, than the other.

The Cochin-chinefe, when preparing the ground for the fugar-cane, turn it up to the depth of two feet;
this

this operation is performed with a plank. They then plant joints or eyes of the cane, three and three together, in a horizontal pofition, in the fame manner almoft as they plant vines in feveral provinces of France. Thefe flips are planted chequer-wife about eighteen inches deep in the ground, diftant fix feet from one another; this operation they perform near the end of the rainy feafon, in order that the flips may be fufficiently watered, till fuch time as they have taken root. During the firft fix months, they give them two dreffings with a kind of pick-axe, in order to deftroy the weeds, and preferve a moifture about the roots of the canes, by heaping the earth around them.

Twelve,

Twelve, and sometimes fourteen, months after the plantation, they gather the first crop. By this time the canes, though planted at the distance of six feet, become so bushy that it is impossible to enter the field, without the assistance of a hatchet to clear your way.

The canes being cut, and tied up into bundles, are carried to the mills, in order to extract their juice. I shall not here describe the form of these machines, which resemble in a great measure those of the West-Indies: instead of water, they employ horned cattle or mules to set in motion the two cylinders, between which the sugar-canes are pressed. These engines have been described by numbers of travellers.

The

The juice being extracted, they boil it some hours in large kettles, in order to evaporate part of its water: it is then transported to the neighbouring market, and sold in that condition. Here ends the industry and the profits of the Cochin-chinese planter. The merchants purchase the juice, which resembles pure water; they boil it again, throwing into the kettles some alkaline substance, such as the ashes of the leaves of the musa or bananier, and shell-lime; they are acquainted with no other; these ingredients throw up a thick scum, which the refiner carefully skims off: the action of the alkali hastens the separation of the salt from the water, and, by the force of ebullition, reduces the juice of the cane to the consistence of syrup. As soon as this syrup

syrup begins to granulate, they decant it into a great earthen veffel, where they cool it about an hour; when a kind of cruft, ftill foft, and of a yellowifh colour, appears on the furface of the fyrup; they lofe not a moment then to empty it into a veffel of a conic fhape, which they call a *form*. Without this intermediate operation of cooling the fyrup, it would harden into a mafs, and not being granulated, would confequently want one effential quality of fugar.

Thefe fugar-cones, or forms, in Cochin-china, are, like thofe of our Weft-India colonies, of baked earth, about three feet high, pierced at their narrow extremities, and contain in general about forty or fifty pounds of fugar. Thefe *forms*, when full, are

are placed on another earthen veffel, the mouth of which is proportioned to receive the narrow end of the cone, and muft be large enough to contain the coarfe fyrup, which diftils from the fugar, through fome ftraw which imperfectly ftops up the little opening in the bottom of the *form*.

When they fuppofe the fyrup has acquired the confiftence of falt in every part of the cone, they then proceed to whiten and purify it. They dilute, in a trough, a fine fort of whitifh clay, with fuch a quantity of water as, when thus prepared, prevents it from having too much confiftence; with a truel they then lay it upon the furface of the fugar to the thicknefs of about two inches, in the void fpace left at the top of the form by the condenfing of the fugar, sugar, after purging itself of the coarser syrup or melasses. The water contained in the clay penetrating by degrees into the mass, washes it, and carries off insensibly the remaining syrup, and every foreign particle that adheres most closely to the sugar. When the clay hardens, they replace it with a fresh quantity, diluted as the first: this operation, which lasts about twelve or fifteen days, is the same here as in our West-India colonies. Some refiners of Cochin-china, however, have another method. In place of clay, tempered thus with water, they cut into small pieces the trunk of the musa or bananier, which they place upon the sugar: the trunk of this tree is very watery; the water of the detergent quality; and distills from the fibres,

which

which envelope it, in very small drops. Those who follow this method pretend, that the operation is thereby rendered less tedious, and that the sugar acquires a finer colour.

The process of the Cochin-chinese, in refining their sugar, goes no further: they are unacquainted with the stoves in use in the West-Indies. After having clayed their sugars sufficiently, they sell them in the public markets, particularly to the Chinese, and other strangers, who are invited to their ports by the moderate price of this commodity, which is cheaper at Cochin-china than any where in India.

The white sugar of the best quality is generally sold at the port of Faifo, in exchange for other merchandize, at the rate of three piaſtres (about fourteen ſhillings) the Cochin-china quintal, which weighs from one hundred and fifty to two hundred pounds French *. The trade in this commodity is immenſe. The Chineſe alone, whoſe lands do not produce enough for their own conſumpt, purchaſe annually from Cochin-china above forty thouſand barrels, weighing about two thouſand pounds per barrel.

This country, it ſhould be obſerved, which produces this commodity in ſuch abundance, and at ſo low a price, being a new kingdom, ought to be conſidered, in ſome meaſure, as a colony : it is worthy obſervation too,

* Ninety-one pounds eight ounces French make one hundred pounds Engliſh.

too, that the fugar-cane is there cultivated by free men, and all the procefs of preparation and refining, the work of free hands. Compare then the price of the Cochin-chinefe production with the fame commodity which is cultivated and prepared by the wretched flaves of our European colonies, and judge if, to procure fugar from our colonies, it was necessary to authorize by law the flavery of the unhappy Africans tranfported to America. From what I have obferved at Cochin-china, I cannot entertain a doubt, but that our Weft-India colonies, had they been diftributed without obfervation amongft a free people, would have produced double the quantity that is now procured from the labour of the unfortunate negroes.

What

What advantage, then, has accrued to Europe, civilized as it is, and thoroughly verſed in the laws of nature, and the rights of mankind, by legally authorizing in our colonies the daily outrages againſt human nature, permitting them to debaſe man almoſt below the level of the beaſts of the field? Theſe ſlaviſh laws have proved as oppoſite to its intereſt as they are to its honour, and to the laws of humanity. This remark I have often made.

Liberty and property form the baſis of abundance, and good agriculture: I never obſerved it to flouriſh where thoſe rights of mankind were not firmly eſtabliſhed. The earth, which multiplies her productions with a kind of profuſion, under the hands of the free-born labourer,

F ſeems

seems to shrink into barrenness under the sweat of the slave. Such is the will of the great author of our nature, who has created man free, and assigned to him the earth, that he might cultivate his possession with the sweat of his brow; but still should enjoy his liberty.

The Cochin-chinese, exclusive of the sugar-cane, employ themselves in the culture of a variety of other productions, of great importance both to their interior fabrics, and external commerce.

They cultivate the cotton-tree, the mulberry, the pepper, the varnish-tree, the date, the tea, the indigo, and the saffron, together with a plant peculiar to the country, called *Tsai*, which, being fermented like indigo,

fur-

furnishes in great plenty a flower of a green colour, which in dying, gives a durable tincture of a fine emerald colour. This plant would undoubtedly be a moſt valuable preſent to our Weſt-India colonies.

I muſt at preſent decline entering into a deſcription of the various proceſſes attending theſe different cultures. They will afford ſubject for ſome future memoirs.

The ſoil in general, of Cochinchina, is excellent, and they cultivate it well. Their mountains in general are fallow, as population is not even ſufficiently conſiderable for the cultivation of all the plain grounds they have taken poſſeſſion of in Camboya: theſe mountains produce, however, the eagle or aloes-wood,

wood, which is the moſt precious perfume in the world; the ſapan-wood, the ſame with that of Braſil; and the cinnamon, in ſmall quantities indeed, but much ſuperior in quality to that of Ceylon.—The Chineſe pay three or four times more for it than for that which the Dutch import from that iſland. They have ſeveral ſorts likewiſe of admirable wood for joyner and cabinet-work, particularly the roſe-wood; the tea-wood is excellent for building, and is preferred to all others in the conſtruction of the royal galleys, having every property that can be wiſhed for either for beauty or ſolidity. From their mountains alſo, and from the foreſts with which they are covered, they procure ivory, muſk, wax, iron, and gold in great abundance. Theſe

moun-

mountains too are full of game, fuch as deer, antelopes, wild goats, peacocks, pheafants, &c. The chace is free to all, but dangerous from the number of tygers, elephants, rhinoceros, and other carnivorous and deftructive animals, with which the forefts abound.

The fea, which wafhes their coafts, as well as the rivers, are well fupplied with excellent fifh. Every one has the liberty of fifhing; and in this the Cochin-chinefe take great delight. I have already obferved, that they live chiefly on fifh and rice.

Their domeftic animals are, the horfe for the road, the buffalo for labour, and the cow, the hog, the goat, the goofe, the duck, and hens of various kinds, for the table. Thefe animals

animals thrive extremely well, and are in great abundance. The king alone referves to himfelf the exclufive right of breeding elephants for the war; and this is a refervation which no man envies him. He maintains generally four hundred of them; he could maintain four thoufand men at a much lefs expence. The Cochinchinefe have few good fruits; the pine-apple, and oranges of different kinds, are the beft their country produces. They do not cultivate the vine, though it is one of the native productions of their lands. They are but indifferently provided with pulfe. In a word, their orchards and their gardens are very inconfiderable. They attach themfelves to the more effential branches of agriculture.

Although

Although this art is not yet arrived at that degree of perfection in Cochin-china, to which it might be carried, with the advantage of such an excellent foil, yet the manners of the people being very favourable, it flourishes greatly. The Cochin-chinefe are gentle, hofpitable, frugal, and induftrious. There is not a beggar in the country; and robbery and murder abfolutely unknown. A ftranger may wander over the kingdom, from one end to another, (the capital excepted) without meeting the flighteft infult : he will be every where received with a moft eager curiofity, but, at the fame time, with great benevolence. I have here remarked a cuftom fingular indeed, but expreffive of their goodnefs of heart. A Cochin-chinefe traveller, who has not money sufficient to defray his expences at an inn, enters the first house of the town or village he arrives at: no body inquires his business; he speaks to none, but waits in silence the hour of dinner;. so soon as the rice is served up, he modestly approaches, places himself at table along with the family, eats, drinks, and departs, without pronouncing a single word, or any person's putting to him a single question: it was enough they saw he was a man, a brother in distress; they asked no further information.

The six first kings, founders of this monarchy, governed the nation as a father governs his family; they established the laws of nature alone; they themselves paid the first obedience to them. Chiefs of an immense
family

family of labourers, they gave the firſt example of labour; they honoured and encouraged agriculture, as the moſt uſeful and honourable employment of mankind. They required from their ſubjects only a ſmall annual free-gift, to defray the expence of their defenſive war againſt their Tonquineſe enemies.

This impoſition was regulated, by way of poll-tax, with the greateſt equity. Every man, able to labour the ground, paid in to the magiſtrate, on account of the prince, a ſmall ſum proportioned to the ſtrength of his conſtitution, and the vigour of his arm; and nothing more. It was under their reign, that this nation multiplied ſo ſurpriſingly, in conſequence of the plenty furniſhed by the culture of their fields. Whilſt they reigned, ed, the treaties entered into, on the banks of the river which feparates Tonquin from Cochin-china, between the chiefs of their family and thofe who followed them in their retreat, were moft religioufly obferved. It is to this reciprocal fidelity that Cochin-china owes its prefent flourifhing ftate, with regard to power, population, and agriculture. Their fucceffor, who now reigns, inherits their goodnefs of heart, but has the weaknefs to fuffer himfelf to be governed by his flaves. Thefe have acquired the art of feparating the intereft of the prince from that of his people. They have infpired him with the thirft after perfonal riches. The vaft quantity of gold which they have dug from the mines, during this reign, has already proved detrimental to induftry and agriculture. In the

the palace it has been productive of luxury and corruption, its never-failing attendants.

This prince has been infenfibly led to defpife the fimple habitations of his anceftors. He has built a fuperb palace, a league in circumference, furrounded by a wall of brick, on the model of that of Pekin. Sixteen hundred pieces of cannon, mounted around the palace, announce to the people the approaching lofs of their liberties and rights.

He found a neceffity too for a winter palace, a fummer palace, and an autumn palace. The old taxes were by no means fufficient to defray thefe expences; they were augmented; and new impofitions devifed, which, being

ing no longer voluntary contributions, could not be levied but by force, and tyrannical oppreffion. His courtiers, who found their intereft in the corruption of their prince, have given him the title of *King of Heaven:* *Vous Tſoi*, hearing himſelf often ſo ſtiled, at length thought he might aſſume it — " Why," addreſſing himſelf one day to me, " don't you " come oftener to pay your court to " the *King of Heaven* ?"

Theſe deſigning ſycophants, who guard every avenue to the royal ear, have had the addreſs to over-awe the ordinary adminiſtration of juſtice; and, taking advantage of exemption from puniſhment, have pillaged the labourers, and filled the provinces with oppreſſion and diſtreſs.

All

All along the high roads I have feen whole villages newly abandoned by their inhabitants, harraffed by fruitlefs toil, and never ending exactions, and their fields, in confequence, falling back to their firft uncultivated ftate.

In the midft of all this growing diforder, the prince, whofe mind has been furprized by fawning flatterers, and who alone is ignorant of the villainy of thofe around him, ftill preferves a refpect for the manners of his anceftors; he does not, indeed, like his forefathers, give an example of perfonal labour, but ftill his defire is to protect agriculture.

I have

I have seen him, at the commencement of the new year, preside, with all the simplicity of his predecessors, at the general assembly of the nation, which is annually held on that day, in the open field, in order to renew the reciprocal oath for observation of the primordial contract, which established him father of his people, at the same time that they invested him alone with the power, the noblest indeed of all, of making his people happy.

When he speaks of his subjects, he calls them still by no other name than that of his children. I have seen him too assist, like a simple individual, in the annual assembly of his family, according to the ancient ufage of the nation; an affembly where the moft aged always prefide, without regard to the dignities of thofe of younger years. This, however, feemed to me only a formality venerable from cuftom; for what is man, where the *King of Heaven* appears?

Corruption, it is true, has not yet infected the general body of the people; they ftill preferve their primitive manners: it is hitherto confined to the palace, and the capital: its fource, however, is too elevated to prevent its poifoned ftreams from flowing to the plains. It is from the great that the corruption of a people ever derives its origin.

When it fhall have infected every rank; when the foundations of agriculture,

culture, liberty and property, already attacked by the great, shall be overthrown; when the profession of the farmer shall become the most contemptible, and the least lucrative, what must be the fate of agriculture? Without a flourishing agriculture, what must be the fate of those multitudes, fostered under its wing?—What must be the fate of prince and people?—It will resemble that of the nation who possessed the country before them; perhaps that of the savages, who yielded it to that nation: of them there are no remains, but the ruins of an immense wall, near the capital, which appears to have been part of a great city: it is of brick, and of a form very different from what is to be seen in the other countries of Asia: no history, however,

no

no tradition has preserved the memory of the builders.

Upon the whole I conclude, from the general corruption which threatens the manners of the Cochin-chinese, that agriculture is on the decline, and that whatever efforts they may make to support it, it has now passed its meridian, and must infallibly degenerate.

C H I N A.

I now approach the period of my travels. Departing from the coasts of Cochin-china, and directing my course towards the north-east, I proceeded for China, which the Cochin-chinese call, with great respect, *Nuse d' ai Ming—the Kingdom of the Great Lumi-*

Luminary. After some days navigation, before there was any appearance of land, I perceived along the horizon a forest of masts, and soon after an innumerable multitude of boats, which covered the surface of the water. These were thousands of fishermen, whose industry drew from the deeps subsistence for numbers. The land now began to rise to my view; I advanced to the mouth of the river, still amidst crowds of fishers, throwing out their lines on every side. I entered the river of Canton; it is peopled like the land; its banks lined with ships at anchor; a prodigious number of small craft are continually gliding along in every direction, some with sails, others with oars, vanishing often suddenly from the sight, as they enter the number-
less

less canals, dug with amazing labour, across extensive plains, which they water and fertilize. Immense fields, covered with all the glory of the harvest, with stately villages rising to the eye on every side, adorn the remoter view, whilst mountains, covered with verdure, cut into terrasses, and shaped into amphitheatres, form the back ground of this noble landscape.

I arrive at Canton, where new subjects for admiration arise; the noise, the motion, the crowd augments; the water, as well as land, being every where covered with multitudes. Astonished at the amazing appearance, I inquire into the numbers of inhabitants of this city and suburbs; and, after comparing different accounts, find that they must amount

at

at least to eight hundred thousand souls. My surprize, however, is greatly increased, when I learn, that, to the northward of Canton, about five leagues up the river, is a village named *Fachan*, which contains a million of inhabitants, and that every part of this great empire, extending about six hundred leagues from north to south, and as much from east to west, was peopled in the same proportion.

By what art can the earth produce subsistence for such numbers? Do the Chinese possess any secret art of multiplying the grain and provisions necessary for the nourishment of mankind? To solve my doubts I traversed the fields, I introduced myself among the labourers, who are in general easy, polite, and affable, with

some

some share of learning, and knowledge of the world. I examine, and pursue them through all their operations, and observe that their secret consists simply in manuring their fields judiciously, ploughing them to a considerable depth, sowing them in the proper season, turning to advantage every inch of ground which can produce the most inconsiderable crop, and preferring to every other species of culture that of grain, as by far the most important.

This system of culture, the last article excepted, appears to be the same that is recommended in all our best authors, ancient and modern, who have wrote on this subject; our common labourers are acquainted with it; but how much must our European farmers be surprized, when they are

in-

informed, that the Chinese have no meadows, natural nor artificial, and have not the least conception of fallowing, never allowing their lands the slightest repose.

The Chinese labourer would consider meadows, of every denomination, as lands in a state of nature; they sow their lands all with grain, and give the preference to such grounds as we generally lay out in meadows, which, lying low, and being properly situated with respect to water, are consequently by far the most fertile. They affirm, that a field sown with grain, will yield as much straw for the nourishment of cattle, as it would have produced of hay, besides the additional advantage of the grain for the sustenance of man, of which they can spare too, in plentiful

tiful seasons, a small portion for the animal creation.

Such is the system adhered to from one extremity of their empire to the other, and confirmed by the experience of four thousand years, amongst a people, of all the nations in the world, the most attentive to their interest.

That which must render this plan of agriculture the more inconceivable to Europeans, is the idea of their never allowing their lands to lie one season unlaboured. Those who for some years have endeavoured, with such public-spirited zeal, to re-animate amongst us this neglected art, have considered, as the first and most important object, the multiplication

of

of artificial meadows, to fupply the defect of natural ones, for the fattening of cattle ; without once venturing to think of fuppreffing the mode of fallowing the grounds, however far they carried their fyftem of increafing the number of artificial paftures.

This fyftem, which appears the moft plaufible of any they have projected, and is received with the greateft partiality by our farmers, is, neverthelefs, contradicted by the conftant experience of the greateft and the moft ancient land-labouring nation in the world, who regard the practice of meadows, and fallowing grounds, as an abufe, deftructive of plenty and population, which are the only important objects of agriculture.

A

A Chinese labourer could not but smile, if you informed him, that the earth has occasion for repose at a certain fixed period of time : he certainly would say, that we deviated greatly from the point in view, could he read our treatises ancient and modern, our marvellous speculations on agriculture : what would he say, if he saw our lands, part of them fallow, part of them employed in useless cultures, and the remainder wretchedly laboured ? What would he say, what must be his feelings, if, in travelling over our fields, he observed the extreme misery and barbarism of their wretched cultivators ?

The Chinese lands, in general, are not superior to ours : you see there, as with us, some excellent grounds, others middling, the rest bad; some soils strong, others light; lands where clay, and lands where sand, gravel, and flints every where predominate.

All these grounds, even in the northern provinces, yield annually two crops, and in those towards the south often five in two years, without one single fallow season, during the many thousands of years that they have been converted to the purposes of agriculture.

The Chinese use the same manures as we do, in order to restore to their grounds those salts and juices, which an unintermitting production is perpetually consuming. They are acquainted with marl; they employ also so common falt, lime, afhes, and all forts of animal dung, but above all that which we throw into our rivers : they make great ufe of urine, which is carefully preferved in every houfe, and fold to advantage : in a word, every thing produced by the earth is re-conveyed to it with the greateft care, into whatever fhape the operations of nature or art may have tranfformed it.

When their manures are at any time fcarce, they fupply the deficiency, by turning up the ground, with the fpade, to a great depth, which brings up to the furface of the field a new foil, enriched with the juices of that which defcends in its room.

Without meadows the Chinese maintain a number of horses, buffaloes, and other animals of every species neceſſary for labour, for ſuſtenance, and for manure. Theſe animals are fed, ſome with ſtraw, others with roots, beans, and grain of every kind. It is true, they have fewer horſes, and horned cattle, in proportion, than we have, yet it is not neceſſary that they ſhould have more.

The whole country is cut into canals, dug by the induſtry of the inhabitants, extending from river to river, which divide and water this vaſt empire, like a garden. Travelling, tranſporting of goods, almoſt every ſpecies of carriage is performed on theſe canals, with great eaſe, and
ſmall

small expence: they don't even use horses to drag their boats; every thing is done by the sail or the oar, which they manage with singular dexterity, even in going up the rivers. Where any kind of labour can be performed, at a moderate price by men, it is a maxim with them never to employ animals. In consequence of this, the banks of their canals are cultivated almost to the water's edge; they lose not an inch of ground: their public roads resemble our foot-paths; their canals, however, are infinitely more useful than highways: they convey fertility every where, and furnish the people great part of their subsistence in fish. — There is no comparison between the weight which can be transported in a boat, and that which can be conveyed by any kind of land-carriage; no proportion between the expence.

The Chinefe are ftill lefs acquainted with the ufe, or rather the luxury of chariots, and equipages of every kind, which crowd the principal cities of Europe. The horfes neceffary for thefe, affembled in thoufands in our capitals, confume the produce of numberlefs acres of our beft grounds, which, if cultivated with grain, would afford fubfiftence for multitudes, who are dying of hunger. The Chinefe wifh rather to maintain men than horfes.

The emperor and chief magiftrates are carried through the cities by men, with fafety and with dignity; their march is fedate and majeftic, it threatens not with danger thofe who
walk

walk on foot : they travel in a kind of galleys, fafer, more commodious, equally magnificent, and lefs expenfive than our land equipages.

I have before obferved, that the Chinefe lofe not an inch of ground. They are very far, therefore, from allotting immenfe parks, of the fineft ground, for the maintenance alone of deer, in contempt of the human race. The emperors, even thofe of the Tartar line, have never hitherto dreamed of forming thefe parks ; ftill lefs the grandees, that is, the magiftrates and the learned : fuch an idea could never find place in the mind of a Chinefe. Even their country houfes, and boxes of pleafure, prefent nothing to the eye all around, but ufeful cultures, agreeably diverfified,

That which conſtitutes their principal beauty, is their delightful ſituation, judiciouſly improved, where, in the diſpoſition of the various parts which form the whole, there every where reigns a happy imitation of that beautiful diſorder of nature, from whence art has borrowed all her charms.

The moſt rocky hills, which, in France, and other places of Europe, they turn into vineyards, or totally neglect, are there compelled, by dint of induſtry, to produce grain. The Chineſe are acquainted, indeed, with the vine, which here and there they plant in arbours; but they conſider it as a luxury, and the wine it produces as an unneceſſary ſuperfluity: they would imagine it a ſin againſt humanity, to endeavour to procure, by by cultivation, an agreeable liquor, whilſt, from the want of that grain which this vineyard might have produced, ſome individual perhaps might be in danger of periſhing of hunger.

The ſteepeſt mountains, even, are rendered acceſſible: at Canton, and from one extremity of the empire to another, you obſerve mountains cut into terraſſes, repreſenting, at a diſtance, immenſe pyramids divided into different ſtages, which ſeem to rear their heads to heaven. Every one of theſe terraſſes yields annually a crop of ſome kind of grain, even of rice; and you cannot with-hold your admiration, when you behold the water of the river, the canal, or the fountain, which glides by the foot of the mountain, raiſed from terraſs to terraſs, even to the ſummit, by means of a simple portable machine, which two men with ease transport and put in motion.

The sea itself, which seems to threaten the solid globe it surrounds, has been compelled, by industry and labour, to yield part of its dominions to the Chinese cultivator.

The two finest provinces of the empire, Nanking and Tché-kiang, formerly covered with water, have been united to the continent some thousands of years ago, with an art infinitely superior to that which is so much admired in the modern works of Holland.

The Chinese had to struggle with a sea, whose natural flux from east to to weſt urges it continually towards the coaſts of theſe two provinces; whilſt the Dutch have had nothing to oppoſe but a ſea, which, by the ſame natural motion, always avoids their weſtern ſhores.

'The Chineſe nation is capable of the moſt ſtupendous works; in point of labour I never obſerved their equals in the world. Every day in the year is a working day, except the firſt, deſtined for paying reciprocal viſits, and the laſt, which is conſecrated to the ceremonial duties they pay to their anceſtors.

An idle man would be treated with the moſt ſovereign contempt, and regarded as a paralytic member, a load to the body of which he made a part; the government would

in

in no manner permit it. How oppofite from the ideas of other Afiatics, where none are admitted to any degree of eftimation, but thofe who, from their fituation in life, have nothing to do!—An ancient emperor of China, in a public inftruction, exhorting the people to labour, obferved, that if in one corner of the empire there was one man who did nothing, there muft, in fome other quarter, be another who fuffers on that account, deprived of the neceffaries of life. This wife maxim is fixed in the breaft of every Chinefe; and, with this people fo open to reafon, he who pronounces a wife maxim pronounces a law.

Behold, gentlemen, a flight fketch of the general picture of Chinefe agriculture, with the peculiar genius of that

that people for this art. The limits of my difcourfe will not permit me at prefent to enter into a detail of the different cultures I have feen in this country: I fhall only obferve, that they are fuch as abundantly fupply all the wants, and conveniencies of the moft populous nation in the world, and furnifh with their fuperfluity, an important article for foreign commerce.

From thefe obfervations it is obvious, that agriculture flourifhes in China more than in any other country in the world: yet it is not to any procefs peculiar to their labour, it is not to the form of their plough, or their method of fowing, that this happy ftate, and the plenty confequent on it, is to be attributed; it muft chiefly be derived from their
mode

mode of government, the immoveable foundations of which have been laid deep, by the hand of reaſon alone, coeval almoſt with the beginning of time; and from their laws, dictated by nature to the firſt of the human race, and ſacredly preſerved from generation to generation, engraved in the united hearts of a great people, not in obſcure codes, deviſed by chicanery and deceit.—In a word, China owes the proſperity of her agriculture to the ſimplicity of her manners, and to her laws, which are the laws of nature and reaſon.

This empire was founded by labourers, in thoſe happy times when the laws of the great Creator were ſtill held in remembrance, and the culture of the earth conſidered as the nobleſt of all employments, the moſt

worthy

worthy of mankind, and the general occupation of all. From *Fou-hi* (who was the firſt chief of this nation, ſome hundreds of years after the deluge, if we follow the verſion of the Septuagint, and in this quality preſided over agriculture) all the emperors, without exception, even to this day, glory in being the firſt labourers of their empire.

The Chineſe hiſtory has carefully preſerved an anecdote of generoſity in two of the ancient emperors, who, not perceiving among their children any one worthy to mount a throne, which virtue alone ought to inherit, named, as their ſucceſſors, two ſimple labourers. Theſe labourers, according to the Chineſe annals, advanced the happineſs of mankind, during very long reigns; their memory is

ſtill

still held in the highest veneration. It is unnecessary to observe how much examples, such as these, honour and animate agriculture.

The Chinese nation has ever been governed like a family, of which the emperor is father: his subjects are his children, without any other inequality but that which is established by talents, and by merits. Those puerile distinctions of *noblesse*, and *plebeians*, *men of family*, and *men of mean birth*, are no where to be found but in the jargon of new people, still barbarous, who, having forgot the common origin of all men, insult without reflection, and debase the whole human race; whilst that nation whose government is ancient, dating its commencement with the first

firſt ages of the world, are ſenſible that all men are born equal, all brothers, all noble. Their language has not even hitherto invented a term for expreſſing this pretended diſtinction of birth. The Chineſe, who have preſerved their annals from the remoteſt times, and who are all equally the children of the emperor, have never ſo much as ſuſpected an inequality of origin amongſt us.

From this principle, that the emperor is father, and the people his children, ſpring all the duties of ſociety, all the duties of morality, every virtue of humanity, the union of every wiſh for the common good of the family, consequently an attachment to labour, and above all to agriculture.

This

This art is honoured, protected, and practised by the emperor, and the great magistrates, who generally are the sons of plain labouring men, whom merit has raised to the first dignities of the empire; and, in a word, by the whole nation, who have the good sense to honour an art the most useful to mankind; in preference to others more frivolous, and less important.

CEREMONY OF OPENING THE GROUNDS.

On the fifteenth day of the first moon, in every year, which generally corresponds to the beginning of March, the emperor in person performs the ceremony of opening the grounds. This prince, in great pomp,

pro-

proceeds to the field appointed for the ceremony : the princes of the imperial family, the prefidents of the five great tribunals, and an infinite number of mandarins accompany him. Two fides of the field are occupied by the emperor's officers, and guards; the third is allotted for all the labourers of the province, who repair thither to behold their art honoured and practifed by the head of their empire; the fourth is referved for the mandarins.

The emperor enters the field alone, proftrates himfelf, and nine times ftrikes his head againft the ground, in adoration of *Tien*, the God of heaven; he pronounces, with a loud voice, a prayer appointed by the tribunal of rites, invoking the bleffing of the almighty fovereign on his labour, and

on

on the labour of his people, who form his family; he then, in quality of sovereign pontiff of the empire, sacrifices a bullock, which he offers up to heaven, as the source of every blessing: whilst they cut the victim in pieces, and place them on the altar, they bring to the emperor a plough, in which are yoked a pair of bullocks, magnificently adorned. The emperor then, laying aside his royal robes, takes hold of the handle of the plough, and turns up several furrows the whole length of the field; then, with a complaisant air, having delivered the plough to the mandarins, they successively follow his example, emulating one another in performing this honourable labour with the greatest dexterity. The ceremony concludes with the distribution of money, and pieces of stuff, among the

the labourers there prefent; the moft
active of whom finifh the remaining
labour, in prefence of the emperor,
with great agility and addrefs.

Some time after, when they have
fufficiently laboured and manured
their grounds, the emperor repairs
again, in proceffion, and begins the
fowing of the fields, always accompanied with ceremony, and attended
by the labourers of the province.

The fame ceremonies are performed, on the fame days in all the provinces of the empire, by the viceroys,
affifted by all the magiftrates of their
departments, in prefence of a great
number of the labourers of their refpective provinces. I have feen this
opening of the grounds at Canton,
and never remember to have beheld

any

any of the ceremonies, invented by men, with half the pleasure and satisfaction with which I observed this.

THE ENCOURAGEMENTS OF AGRICULTURE.

The Chinese agriculture has, at the same time, other encouragements. Every year the viceroys of the provinces send to court the names of such labourers as have chiefly distinguished themselves in their employments, either by cultivating grounds till then considered as barren, or, by a superior culture, improving the production of such lands as formerly had bore grain. These names are presented to the emperor, who confers on them honorary titles, to distinguish them above their fellow-labourers. If any man has made an

impor-

important difcovery, which may influence the improvement of agriculture, or fhould he, in any manner, deferve more diftinguifhed marks of regard than the reft, the emperor invites him to Pekin, defraying his journey, with dignity, at the expence of the empire; he receives him into his palace, interrogates him with regard to his abilities, his age, the number of his children, the extent and quality of his lands; then difmiffes him to his plough, diftinguifhed by honourable titles, and loaded with benefits and favours.

Who is happieft, gentlemen, the prince who conducts himfelf in this manner, or the nation who is thus governed? Amongft a people where all are equal, where every one afpires after

after diftinctions, fuch encouragements cannot fail to infpire a love for labour, and an emulation for the cultivation of the ground.

ATTENTION OF THE CHINESE GOVERNMENT.

The whole attention, in general, of the Chinefe government, is directed towards agriculture. The principal object of the father of a family, ought to be the fubfiftence of his children. The ftate of the fields, in confequence forms the great object of the toils, the cares, and the folicitudes of the magiftrates. It may eafily be conceived, that, with fuch difpofitions, the government has not neglected to fecure to the labourers that liberty, property, and indul-
gence

gence which are the great fprings for the improvement of agriculture.

The Chinefe enjoy, undifturbed, their private poffeffions, as well as thofe which, being by their nature indivifible, belong to all, fuch as the fea, the rivers, the canals, the fifh which they contain, and the beafts of the foreft : navigation, fifhing, and the chace are free to every one ; and he who buys a field, or receives it by inheritance from his anceftors, is of courfe the fole lord and mafter.

The lands are free as the people ; no feudal fervices, and no fines of alienation ; none of thofe men inte-refted in the misfortunes of the pub-lic ; none of thofe farmers who never amafs more exorbitant fortunes, than when an unfavourable feafon has ruin-

H   ed

ed the country, and reduced the unhappy labourer to perish for want, after having toiled the year round for the suftenance of his fellow subjects; none of that deftructive profeffion, hatched in the delirium of the feudal fyftem, under whofe aufpices arife millions of proceffes, which drag the labourer from his plough into the obfcure and dangerous mazes of chicane, and thereby rob him while defending his rights, of that time which would have been importantly employed in the general fervice of mankind.

THE IMPOSTS ESTABLISHED IN CHINA INVARIABLE.

In China there is no other lord, no other fuperior, who has power to levy taxes, but the common father of the family, the emperor. The bonzes

zes (priefts of the fect of Fo-hi) accuftomed to receive alms from a charitable people, would be very indifferently received, fhould they pretend that this alms is a right which heaven has beftowed upon them.

THE IMPOST CALLED THE TENTH.

This impoft, which is not exactly the tenth part of the produce, is regulated according to the nature of the grounds : in bad foils it is perhaps only the thirtieth part, and fo in proportion. This impoft, however, of the tenth part of the produce of the earth, which belongs to the emperor, is the only tax on the lands, the only tribute known in China fince the origin of the monarchy ; and fuch is the happy refpect which the Chinefe have for their ancient cuſtoms, that an emperor of China would never entertain the moſt diſtant thought of augmenting it, nor his ſubjects the leaſt apprehenſion of ſuch augmentation. The people pay it, in kind, not to avaricious farmers-generals, but to upright magiſtrates, their proper and natural governors. The amount of this tribute, though apparently trifling, muſt be immenſe, when we conſider that it is levied on every foot of ground of the moſt extenſive and beſt cultivated empire in the world. This tax is paid with the greateſt fidelity, as they know the purpoſes to which it is applied. They know, that part of it is laid up in immenſe magazines, diſtributed over every province of the empire, and allotted for the maintenance of the magiſtrates and

fol-

foldiery : they know, that, in the event of fcarcity, thefe magazines are open to all, and the wants of the people fupplied with part of that which was received from them in times of abundance : they know too, that the remainder of this impoft is fold in the public markets, and the produce of it faithfully carried to the treafury of the empire, the cuftody of which is intrufted to the refpectable tribunal of *Ho-pou*, from whence it never is iffued but to fupply the general wants of the family.

COMPARISON OF THE AGRICULTURE OF AFRICA AND ASIA WITH THAT OF CHINA.

Recollect, gentlemen, what I have faid of the laws, the manners, and the cuftoms of the different nations of Africa and Afia, the ftate of whofe agriculture I have examined: compare nation with nation, and then judge, if the unfortunate Malabar, without property, fubjected to the tyrannical government of the Moguls; judge if a race of flaves, under the iron fcepter of the defpote of Siam; judge if the Malais, ever turbulent, and fettered by their feudal laws; judge, I fay, if thefe nations, though poffeffing the fineft grounds in the world, can poffibly ever

ever make agriculture to flourish like the Chinese, governed as a family, and subjected to the laws of reason alone.—I shall again repeat, therefore, with confidence, that, in every country in the world, the fate of agriculture depends solely on the laws there established, on the manners of the people, and even on the prejudices which derive their origin from those laws.

What industry hath the inhabitants of the earth displayed, from one extremity of the globe to the other, in rendering themselves unhappy! Created to live in society, to cultivate the earth, and enjoy from their labour the infinite blessings of the great Creator, they had only to listen to the voice of nature, who would have taught them happiness below: in place of of which, they have ftrained their faculties in the invention of barbarous inftitutions, and perplexing legiflations, which being ill adapted to the feelings of mankind, and difcordant with that law which is engraved in every man's breaft, their eftablifhment could only be effected by force, deluging the world with blood ; and which, once eftablifhed, have continued to defolate the earth, checking population, by the oppreffion of agriculture.

THE STATE OF AGRICULTURE IN EUROPE.

What an object for an attentive traveller, to obferve the ftate of agriculture amongft the various people who divide the globe ! In Europe behold it at prefent flourifhing, in a country which, during many preceding ages was reduced to the neceſſity of begging ſubſiſtence amongſt the neighbouring nations, who poſſeſſed a happier climate, and a greater extent of territory. During thoſe ages of barbariſm, their loſs of liberty and right of property brought along with them the ruin of cultivation ; nor has ſhe recovered thoſe natural rights of mankind, and re-eſtabliſhed the foundations of drooping agriculture, but through ſeas of blood, and outrages ſhocking to humanity.

IN AFRICA.

Africa, in general, whoſe regions, known to the ancients, were conſidered as the granaries of the world, now preſent nothing to the view but grounds

grounds either intirely neglected, or wretchedly cultivated by the labour of slaves.

IN AMERICA.

South - America, covered with marshes, brambles, and woods, beholds her extensive tracks hardened even by the sweat of her labourers in chains. The northern regions of that quarter of the world are inhabited by inconsiderable tribes of savages, miserable, and without culture; yet free, and, in consequence, less wretched perhaps than those nations who pretend to be civilized; but who, being farther removed from the laws of nature, by the privation of those rights which she bestows, make ineffectual efforts to procure that happiness, pinefs, which a good agriculture alone can produce.

IN ASIA.

The vaft continent of Afia offers to your confideration, in one quarter, an immenfe uncultivated region, peopled by a race of banditti, more intent on plunder than the cultivation of their grounds; in another, a great empire, formerly flourifhing, and excellently laboured, now inhabited by the poor remains of a wretched people, perifhing with hunger from the neglect of agriculture, and fhedding their blood, not for liberty but for a change of tyrants. This charming fertile quarter of the world (the cradle of the human race) now beholds her lands in flavery, her labourers in chains, fubjected either

to

to the blind defpotifm of unfeeling tyrants, or the deftructive yoke of the feudal fyftem.

But turn your eyes to the eaftern extremity of the Afiatic continent, inhabited by the Chinefe, and there you will conceive a ravifhing idea of the happinefs the world might enjoy, where the laws of this empire the model of thofe of other countries. This great nation unites under the fhade of agriculture, founded on liberty and reafon, all the advantages poffeffed by whatever nation, civilized or favage. The blefling pronounced on man, at the moment of his creation, feems not to have had its full effect, but in favour of this people, who have multiplied as the fands on the fhore.

Princes,

Princes, who rule over nations! arbiters of their fate! view well this perfpective; it is worthy your attention. Would you wifh abundance to flourifh in your dominions, would you favour population, and make your people happy; behold thofe innumerable multitudes which overfpread the territories of China, who leave not a fhred of ground uncultivated; it is liberty, it is their undifturbed right of property that has eftablifhed a cultivation fo flourifhing, under the aufpices of which this people have increafed as the grains which cover their fields.

Does the glory of being the moft powerful, the richeft, and the happieft of fovereigns touch your ambition, turn your eyes towards Pekin,
and

and behold the moſt powerful of mortal beings ſeated on the throne of reaſon :—he does not command, he inſtructs ;—his words are not decrees, they are the maxims of juſtice and wiſdom ;—his people obey him, becauſe his orders are dictated by equity alone.

He is the moſt powerful of men, reigning over the hearts of the moſt numerous ſociety in the world, who conſtitute his family. — He is the richeſt of ſovereigns, drawing from an extent of territory ſix hundred leagues ſquare, cultivated even to the ſummits of the mountains, the tenth of thoſe abundant harveſts it inceſſantly produces : this he conſiders as the wealth of his children, and he huſbands it with care.—To ſum up all, he is the happieſt of monarchs,

taſting

tasting every day the inexpressible pleasure of giving happiness to millions, and alone enjoying, undivided, that satisfaction which his subjects share—his children! all to him equally dear; all living like brothers, in freedom and abundance, under his protection.

He is called the son of *Tien*, as the true and most perfect image of heaven, whose benevolence he imitates; and his grateful people adore him as a God, because his conduct is worthy of a Man.

F I N I S.

www.ingramcontent.com/pod-product-compliance
Lightning Source LLC
Chambersburg PA
CBHW032143160426
43197CB00008B/758